JOHN HUNGERF

A DESCRIPTION

OF

THE TRAJAN COLUMN

THE TRAJAN COLUMN.

THE COLUMN OF TRAJAN.

As it is seen through the excavations of the Ulpian Basilica from the Forum of Trajan.

SCIENCE AND ART DEPARTMENT
OF THE COMMITTEE OF COUNCIL ON EDUCATION,
SOUTH KENSINGTON MUSEUM.

A DESCRIPTION

OF

THE TRAJAN COLUMN.

BY

JOHN HUNGERFORD POLLEN, M.A.,

CORRESPONDING MEMBER, R.A., MADRID, ETC.;
)ITOR AND REFEREE, S. AND A. DEPT., SOUTH KENSINGTON MUSEUM.

LONDON:
PRINTED BY GEORGE E. EYRE AND WILLIAM SPOTTISWOODE,
PRINTERS TO THE QUEEN'S MOST EXCELLENT MAJESTY.
AND SOLD BY CHAPMAN & HALL,
AGENTS TO THE DEPARTMENT FOR THE SALE OF EXAMPLES,
193, PICCADILLY, LONDON.
1874.

LIST OF WOODCUTS.

The Department is indebted to Messrs. George Bell and Sons for the loan of the woodcut used for the frontispiece. The woodcut of the bridge is repeated at p. 160.

A 4

THE TRAJAN COLUMN.

In the following description of the Trajan Column there is no attempt to give a complete account of Roman arms, accoutrements, or warlike engines, nor more of the history of Trajan than is required to illustrate the wars portrayed on his column, and the more important architectural structures erected during his reign.

The casts, which form the subject of these pages, are taken from a series reproduced in metal by direction of the late Emperor Napoleon the Third, and are built round a core of brick in the South-east Court of the South Kensington Museum.

INTRODUCTION.

THE Trajan Column stands on one side of the great Ulpian basilica or hall in the forum built by Trajan, and called after the name of that emperor. Its position is shown in the accompanying plan. On two sides of it stood libraries, one for Greek and one for Latin books. The fronts of these are perhaps indicated by the colonnades which surrounded the column on two sides, as may be seen by the foundations still remaining in the forum. A third row, or foundations of a third colonnade, can be traced at the same distance from the column, on the side furthest from the basilica.

Beyond the column stood the temple erected and dedicated (at a later period, perhaps by his adopted son Hadrian) to Trajan. It would seem as if, independently of the two libraries and temple, there may have been a colonnade surrounding the column as described above ; the foundations of three rows of columns can be traced corresponding with each other in the spaces of inter-columniation, as well as in size and distance from the sides of the pedestal of the great column.

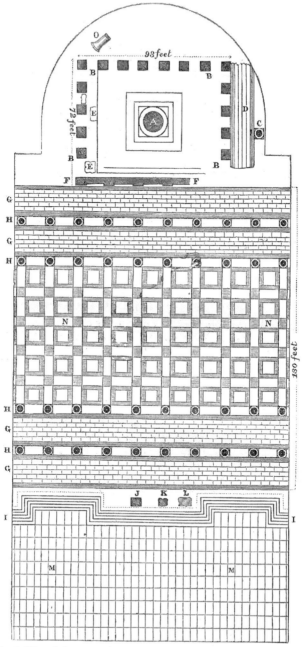

Fig. 1. Plan of the excavations of the forum of Trajan in Rome (reduced from Taylor and Cressy).

EXPLANATION OF THE PLAN.

A. The column.

B, B, B, B. Colonnade round the column.

C. Remains of a single column.

D. Pavement round colonnade.

E, E. Square bases.

F, F. West wall of basilica.

G, G, G, G. Pavement of colonnades inside the basilica.

H, H, H, H. Four rows of columns that supported the roof.

I, I. Steps leading from the forum.

J, K, L. Fragments of bases.

M. Pavement of open forum.

N. Pavement of the central part of basilica.

O. Fragment of a column.

· The front of the great Ulpian basilica formed the western side of the forum of Trajan, an oblong enclosure surrounded by a covered colonnade walled on the outer side, and having an entrance under a triumphal arch in the middle of its eastern side, that opposite the basilica. The statue of Trajan on horseback, in gilt bronze, stood in the middle of the forum, and the actions of Trajan were commemorated in several groups of bronze or marble. The balustrades and many adjuncts and portions of these buildings were decorated with gilded images of arms, horses, &c.

The whole was designed by Apollodorus, an architect who was employed by the emperor Trajan and the senate, not only in the construction of the forum, basilica, and later of the temple ;[1] but his engineering powers were best illustrated in the bridge or bridges which he threw over the Danube, the greatest achievement probably in that kind of construction brought to completion by any nation of antiquity. There is little known of him ; classical biographers name Damascus as his birthplace. He is said to have been put to death by Hadrian.[2]

Though Apollodorus was the architect and sculptor chosen by the emperor, it is more than probable that much of the outline of these vast undertakings was suggested by Trajan himself. That emperor was a careful general and a valiant soldier rather than a man of letters or a connoisseur in art. " It may be presumed," says Merivale, " that an officer who was deemed qualified to become prætor and consul had enjoyed the ordinary advantages of training in *rhetoric* " (it will be seen in examining the bas-reliefs of the column that Trajan was fond of oratory) " and literature ; but Trajan's attainments in learning were slender, and modesty or discretion led him to conceal deficiencies rather than to affect accomplishments he did not possess."[3] Nevertheless it is difficult to suppose that the emperor was without a real love of art, and appreciated more than any ruler of Rome the magnificence of the scale both in size and splendour of material to which Roman architecture had attained, and which he did so much to increase. Both the basilica and the column reached the utmost that was possible in architecture in these respects, and are justly reckoned as the last successful efforts of classic art. His buildings were badly copied or actually robbed, as in the case of the triumphal arch of Constantine, by the architects of future emperors.

---

[1] Dion Cassius, lxix. 4.   [2] Out of jealousy, but the story is open to doubt.
[3] Merivale, Rome under the Emperors, lxiii.

Besides erecting these great buildings, Trajan accomplished the desire of former improvers of Rome, often partially attempted, as in the *fora* of Cæsar or Augustus ; and of Nerva, that of opening a way round the Capitoline hill into the flat ground of the Campus Martius behind. He cut away accordingly a tongue of land that united the portion of the Capitoline, now occupied by the church of the Aracæli, with the Quirinal. The exact proportions of the column were so arranged as to show what height of ground had been cut away in finding a level for the forum, basilica, and temple beyond, as will be seen in the description of the base of the column. As regards the scale of the whole of these buildings the breadth of the Ulpian basilica has been ascertained by the excavations made in the early part of this century : it is given as 183 feet by Taylor and Cressy in the ' Architectural antiquities of Rome.' The length has not been explored, as the ground lies over it to a depth of 15 feet. Canina gives the total length, including absidal ends, at about three diameters and the length or area of the forum at about two diameters of the basilica, *i.e.*, at between 300 and 400 feet. The columns of the basilica are noble blocks of Egyptian granite, 3 feet $8\frac{2}{10}$ inches in diameter. The triumphal arch, which gave entrance to the forum, was the last commemoration of the triumph of Trajan after his Dacian wars and the subsequent warlike achievements of his reign, and was not completed till after his death.

The column was specially intended as the personal monument and tomb of the emperor, wherein his ashes were laid, an honour exceptionally decreed to him by the senate, as all intramural burials were contrary to law. The bas-reliefs round the shaft commemorate only one of his war-like achievements, viz., the conquest of Decebalus and the annexation of the whole of Dacia to the empire as a Roman province, after two difficult and bloody wars. Throughout these sculptures we trace the character of the emperor, and a detailed description of a notable portion of his life. He is held up by the historians of the imperial ages as the type of the military hero, as such a type was measured by the Romans of his day, yet with the exception of the sculptures about to be described no history of the life and actions of Trajan has survived. Pliny, the younger, has left behind him a number of letters addressed to the emperor on questions connected with his government of Bithynia, and a panegyric which he pronounced in the autumn of the year 100. In it are compliments to some of his known good qualities, anecdotes or allusions to his military powers, his patience and humanity, but not much

material for history. The poet, Caninius Rufus, projected an epic in praise of the Dacian war, but it was never
completed. The Augustan history, the work of several
authors, begins with the reign of Hadrian, the successor of
Trajan. The part of the history of Dion Cassius which
treats of the reign of Trajan has been lost, and survives
only in the abridgement of Xiphilinus ; and of the commen-
taries on the war, written by the emperor himself, there
remain but fragments which, however, are just sufficient
to confirm the evidence we have from other sources of one
of the lines of march from the Danube into Transylvania.[4]

Great, therefore, as the place is that Trajan holds in
Roman history by his character, his military accomplishments, and his virtues, we know less of him from the Roman
historians than of his degenerate successors, and hence the
Trajan column, with its sculptured bas-reliefs, is of excep-
tional importance as a contemporary pictorial record.
And as the province of Dacia was one of the last great
conquests and acquisitions of the empire, and amongst the
most carefully ruled and colonized as long as the great
emperor lived, such an authentic record of the war is of
value, quite apart from its interest as a monument of Roman
art. Dacia was abandoned by Hadrian, who broke down
the bridge that connected that country with the southern
bank of the Danube.[5]

---

[4] " It is sincerely to be lamented that whilst we are fatigued with the dis-
gustful relation of Nero's crimes and follies, we are reduced to collect the
actions of Trajan from the glimmerings of an abridgement, or the doubtful
light of a panegyric."—Gibbon, iii.

[5] According to Dion, though there seem reasons to doubt the truth of his
statement. Merivale, ch. lxvi.

Fig. 2.

From a bust in the British Museum.

M. ULPIUS TRAJANUS IMPERATOR.

The school in which the conqueror of Dacia was formed was the command of the Roman army, still an instrument of power without a rival ; in distant provinces far removed from the dangerous influences that made the prætorian guard in Rome a source of danger to the emperor, the senate, and the people. The Ulpian family is reputed to have been ancient. It was supposed to have been transplanted into Spain from Italy when Scipio Africanus founded a colony at Italica on the Bœtis. Here the family gave birth to many persons of note, amongst them to Trajanus, the father of the emperor. Trajanus commanded the tenth legion at the bloody storming of Joppa. He became proconsul of Asia. As Pliny, in his panegyric, A.D. 100, alludes to him as dead but not yet deified by the emperor, it is supposed that his death had not long happened, and that he survived the elevation of his son to the imperial dignity.

Trajan the emperor was born about A.D. 53, and was elected emperor about his 45th year. He had been trained in the camp under his father, with whom he served in his Parthian campaign in 67, and had won the confidence and love of the legions from his youth. He had held the post of military tribune for ten years, and while

serving in this rank he had learnt the names, and had
witnessed the services and the wounds[6] of both officers
and soldiers subsequently placed in distant garrisons.
He seems to have shown talents for civil administration
as well as war, and like some of our great modern commanders he was called to the capital in the intervals of war
to fill civil appointments at home. He was made prætor;
was afterwards in command in Spain; from Spain he was
sent to quell the revolt of L. Antonius Saturninus in Upper
Germany (the revolt, however, had been already sup-
pressed when he reached Germany) ; he was consul in 91,
and afterwards sent to a government in Germania Superior.
Here he ruled with firmness, and kept the border tribes
under control. He seems to have shown not only great
military experience and skill in his German government,
but to have given proofs of a loyal fidelity to the emperor
and the senate, and of his capacity for the difficult and
important services he could render to the empire, in not
only subduing, but attaching rich and important de-
pendencies, inhabited by vigorous and valiant tribes, who
could add to the security and wealth as well as recruit the
legions of the state. It was to these various qualities,
and to his popularity with the legions, that Trajan owed
his adoption by Nerva, a just and merciful Emperor, but
too old to stand alone and not strong enough to ensure the
tranquil accession of a successor.

Trajan left on the Rhine, and in the states between that
river and the Danube, enduring memorials of his skill in
military engineering. He built Ulpia Trajana, a military
town that bore his name for centuries. He threw a bridge
across the Rhine at Mainz, as Julius Cæsar had done lower
down the river, and we shall have to compare the structure
of the latter with that thrown over the Danube below the
Iron gates. He planted a colony 10 miles beyond the river
at Hochst,[7] and another at Aquæ, or Aurelia Aquenus, the
medical springs of the modern Baden Baden. He seems to
have completed the lines of Drusus and Tiberius, which ran
across the Taunus in an oblique direction from the banks
of the river opposite to Bonn, and to have entertained the
notion of a rampart from the Rhine to the Danube, a
design carried out by degrees by several of his successors,
and of which traces can be made out still from river to
river.[8]

---

[6] Pliny, Panegyr. 15   [7] Mannert, Geogr. iii. 463.
    [8] See a detailed account of the Limes Rhœticus and Limes Transrhenanus, by
Mr. Yates, in the Proceedings of the Archæological Institute, 1852, vol. 2.

Trajan made his entry into Rome in the year 99, as soon as matters were satisfactorily disposed for the security of the empire in this quarter. He had been honoured with the title of Germanicus and the name of Nerva, his father, on his adoption; and he had been nominated consul for the second time before the death of Nerva, but had declined to accept it on account of his residence abroad. His entry into Rome was remarkable. " He had made no exactions from the provinces as was usual on such occasions. Pliny describes the condescension and affability of the prince, who entered the capital on foot unattended by guards, distinguished only by the height of his stature and the dignity of his bearing; he allowed citizens of all ranks to throng about him; returned the greetings of the senators on his return as emperor, with the same kind familiarity with which he had accepted them when he set forth as a fellow-subject; addressing the knights by name; paying his vows to the gods in the Capitol; and entering the palace of the Cæsars as the modest owner of a private mansion."[9] His wife Plotina and his sister Marciana, who gave her name to one of the military stations in Dacia, were worthy associates of the great emperor, and maintained along with him the same magnanimous behaviour from the beginning to the end of his reign.

Trajan remained in Rome two years settling important matters. He punished the delators; reduced the privileges of the prætorians, and reformed the law courts. He earned the title of Optimus. It was, according to Eutropius, the custom of after ages to salute an emperor as more fortunate than Augustus and better than Trajan [10] but the title of Best was one never given to any other emperor, though all other epithets and titles were transmitted from father to son. It was in the fourth year of his reign that he left Rome for his Dacian wars. He was eager to make use of an army trained with so much care under his own eye, and he also conceived that war was in some sort the mission and business of Rome, and that his own title to hold and transmit the imperial crown would be consolidated by military exploits, an opinion in which he has had many successors in modern times.

---

[9] Merivale from Pliny, Pan. 22, &c.   [10] Eutrop. viii. 5.

THE DACIANS.

The Dacians were a powerful race. They had learnt the
art of war in their contests against Domitian, during
whose reign they had not only won advantages over the
legions, but had by bribery or force obtained warlike
engines and Roman artificers capable of constructing these
pieces, who were carefully watched in the interior of the
country. Their dresses, arms, vases of gold and silver,
their *oppida* and fortifications, in some instances the vessels
in which chiefs who came over to the Romans are represented as bringing food and stores, show that they were
very different from the German allies and tributaries of
Rome. Evidences of such a kind abound throughout the
bas-reliefs of the column. Their metallurgy seems little
inferior to that of the Romans though they fight without
armour; exposing their bodies, covered only with their
ample linen tunics and cloaks, to the mail-clad *triarii*
and *principes*, the armoured ranks of the Roman legions.
They were a branch of the Getæ, a people of whom it
was remarked "that they stood nearest to the Greeks
in their natural aptitude for civilization." The Getæ
were settled south of the Danube in Bulgaria and partly
in Roumelia. The Dacians had crossed the Danube, and
had overrun Wallachia, Transylvania, Moldavia, the Banat
and parts of Hungary as far westward as the river Theiss.
From the Theiss on the west they reached to the Pruth on
the east, and the Carpathians on the north. They seem
to have chosen as the seat of government in the second
century the central mountain region of the spurs of the
western Carpathians. Those mountains form an almost
continuous barrier round Transylvania, and in the south-
western portion of that country, on a rocky eminence,
Decebalus the king fortified his capital Zarmizegethusa.
    The entrance to the fertile region on which these hills
look down is closed by formidable passes easily defended ;
by those of the Irongate, (not the Iron gates of the Danube),
of the Rothenthurm, and others. The basin of the Maros
was protected by these mountain barriers, and about their
fertile slopes were the chief towns of the Dacians. Other
rivers, affluents of the Theiss and the Danube, such as the
Tisia or Temes, the Aluta, and the Schyl, also take their rise
amongst these mountains. The country not only abounded
in well watered pastures, on which countless herds of cattle
of all kinds and flocks of sheep were fed, as is shown in

various portions of the sculptures on the column; but it possessed rich mines of gold, silver, and iron. Such a country was worth conquest and annexation on account of its agricultural and mineral wealth alone, even if no political motives had intervened to add to its importance as a frontier defence to the empire.

DECEBALUS.

Decebalus was the name of the monarch who had united the scattered tribes of this pastoral country. Duras and other princes of the country had been either dethroned or united as allies or dependants, and a number of tribes or races had been moulded in some sense by this monarch into one powerful nation. The most important people, and that found most difficult of subjugation by Decebalus, seem to have been the Jazyges, a race originally inhabiting parts of the Roman province of Mœsia, south of the Danube. From thence they had been transplanted or driven out by the Romans, to those portions of Hungary that lie east and west of the Theiss, and they are known as Jazyges Metanastæ from this emigration. Decebalus did not succeed in annexing or in forming a very permanent coalition with the Jazyges, but he seems to have tried to do so, and his attempt on their territory at a later period furnished one of the arguments for the second Dacian war.

Decebalus, under Domitian, had proved a formidable enemy to the Romans. From the mountain region already named he seems to have issued forth on many occasions, more especially during winter, when the marshy ground on the Wallachian shore of the Danube was passable for his cavalry, and even the river itself in severe seasons was scarcely an impediment, being frozen or covered with floating ice, while the Roman vessels of war were during such a season no protection. Such an exploit against one of the Roman stations is perhaps represented in No. XXII. of the bas-reliefs of the column. He made sudden attacks on these Roman stations, carried off treasure, arms and what was of greater importance, Roman artificers, and then crossing the whole breadth of Wallachia, he put the mountain barriers of Transylvania between himself and the Romans, and the length of the Banat between his capital and the mouth of the Save, on which the arsenals of the empire were built. The Emperor Domitian was too weak to keep in order a border country so wide in extent, or to bring under a king or chieftain so valiant, so well followed and with so many material resources, in arms, machines and treasure. Julianus, the general sent by Domitian to oppose this potentate, seems to have been frequently worsted in open fight, and that the superiority of the Roman arms was seriously lowered in these wars there can be no doubt.

The Dacians were as well armed in some respects as the legionaries, for we hear of Julianus ordering his soldiers to write their names and those of their several centurions upon their shields, so that his men might be distinguished when covered by them from the enemy.[11] Julianus did at last gain a victory of real importance at Tapæ, in which the loss of the Dacians is said to have been so severe, that the officer second in command, Vezinas, had to throw himself amongst his own dead to escape notice, and crept out and made his retreat after night fall. Some show of vigorous pursuit was made on this occasion, as the Romans pressed forward to storm the stronghold of Decebalus. That leader prepared his defence by making, amongst other means of protection, dummy soldiers of wood, which he placed behind stockades, and in advantageous positions in the forest country, to frighten the pursuers.[12] Altogether this battle seems to have been but a casual piece of success, and the Roman general can hardly be supposed to have followed up the fugitives with real earnestness of purpose, if such resources were used against him. The slaughter was nevertheless considerable, and Julianus seized the occasion to send a number of heads to Rome, where the ghastly trophies were exposed before the rostra in the forum.[13]

The emperor Domitian took the opportunity to give himself a triumph at Rome, decorating the procession with spoils not really captured in war, but brought for the purpose out of the imperial armouries in Rome.[14] He consented, nevertheless, to a peace with the Dacian king, and to the payment of an annual tribute. To purchase peace at such a sacrifice was not only dishonourable, it was not safe for the empire. Domitian was succeeded by Nerva, who had neither military power nor physical vigour to prosecute a new war, but under Trajan it had become a necessity. The emperor had not only the eagerness of a soldier for war out of the love of enterprise, and the desire of glory ; but he was also well aware of the danger to the state, threatened by all the circumstances already detailed, and he knew both himself and his army well enough to have little doubt as to the issue of the war he proposed to undertake himself.

---

[11] Dion Cassius, lxvii.   [12] *Ibid.*   [13] *Ibid.*   [14] *Ibid.*

5γ

. *The army which the Emperor Trajan collected for the war.*

The army considered sufficient for the contemplated war consisted of seven legions, viz., the first, the 'Minervia,' the second, the 'Adjutrix,' called also the 'Pia,' and at a later period of the war, 'Trajana.' After the war this legion was stationed in Lower Germany. The second legion at the end of the war received the decorations of a mural crown, and was raised to the equestrian rank. Inscriptions show that the fourth, fifth, seventh, and eleventh, took part in each war. The thirteenth legion seems to have had some share in the expedition, though not actually engaged in the campaign. It was left in reserve in Pannonia, through which country the emperor marched to the theatre of the war. The sixth and thirteenth[15] legions both congratulated the fortunate commander on his personal safety. Inscriptions also indicate that other legions, such as the tenth and fifteenth, took some part, probably the charge of the fortified stations and river side ports of the Save and the Danube, which served as reserves and defences of the base of operations. Many of the corps employed were drawn from the army Trajan had already trained so well on the Rhine. To these complete legions were added ten cohorts of prætorians, a *corps d'élite*. They were raised in this instance from the whole Roman army. "They are known," says Francke, "in the sculptures we are about to examine, by their clasping hands and by their raised fingers, in token of mutual fidelity."[16] In No. XXX. are shown two men embracing, brothers perhaps, who belong to cohorts drawn from different legions, meeting after a bloody engagement. In No. XXVI. will be seen the action of raising the forefinger.

Besides these highly disciplined regular troops, numbers of auxiliaries, some of whom were Germans, were employed by Trajan, who knew what their qualifications were, and how far he could depend on them.

The constitution and divisions of the Roman legions had undergone much change since the date of the wars of the Republic. Detailed descriptions of the armies and distribution of parts in the legions of the imperial ages, are to be gathered from the doubtful authority of Vegetius Renatus.[17] The general account which he gives is confused, but his writings contain a number of traditions and minute details which are illustrated in many parts of these bas-reliefs.

[15] Orellius, ii. 3048.   [16] Francke, Gesch. des leben Trajans, p. 95.
[17] Vegetii Renati de re Militari.

THE LEGION.

The name of legion was derived from the custom of choosing, *legere*, the officers and men who made up those bodies and, though many changes in their constitution took place, the title survived down to the time of the removal of the seat of empire. The bodies of men so named did not answer to any modern military organization in the armies of our own times. They were larger than regiments, and were composed of all the arms of the service. They were in fact what would now make small *corps d'armée*, containing infantry, which formed the main strength of Roman armies as of those of the present day ; with a proportion of cavalry ; of artillery, such as was then in use ; and of sappers and engineers. Each Roman legion was thus a complete army, carried its own baggage, reserve stores of arms and ammunition, provisions, tools for camping, mining, fortifications ; and amongst the men were found armourers, smiths, masons and carpenters, latterly boat-builders. The legion was competent to engage the enemy on any ground, to conduct sieges, make temporary or permanent entrenchments, and could be settled as a border colony on suitable sites, where the soldiers began forthwith to construct walled towns, temples, baths, theatres, etc. They will be often seen so employed in the bas-reliefs.

The old constitution of the legion numbered 4,000 or 4,200 infantry, 300 cavalry, 150 officers, 75 standard bearers ; in all 4,725. The number of the infantry at various times exceeded 4,000, and from the second consulship of Marius was about 5,000, and under the empire 6,000 and 6,200 ; 5,000 however was generally the limit of this larger number. The cavalry seems not to have increased but to have diminished to less than half the old number during the centuries of imperial rule, and its employment to have been confined to outpost duty, reconnaissances, etc., during the campaigns of the emperors. In the course of these sculptures, however, the cavalry are often seen engaged in attacking close formations and in pursuing the broken bodies of Dacians, sometimes galloping through and firing the towns or settlements through which they chase the enemy, and hunting up refugees amongst the mountain defiles round Sarmizegethusa and other *oppida* in and about the valley to which the Irongate, the Vulkan, Rothenthurm, and other passes had given the Romans access.

SUBDIVISIONS OF THE LEGION.

The legion was divided, originally, according to the age and period of service of the men. The younger soldiers were *velites* and were formed into *manipuli* or companies, a name taken from the *handful* of grass or fern which was tied to a lance and served as an ensign. There were fifteen *manipuli* of *hastati*, each containing sixty men, two *centuriones* and one *vexillarius* or standard bearer. They formed the front line in action or on the march. Behind the *hastati* came the *principes*, older soldiers composed in the same manner; behind the *principes* the *triarii* composed of the best and steadiest veterans in the legion. They also were in the same formation as the first two lines, viz. fifteen companies, but each containing three *manipuli*, that is one hundred and eight privates, six centurions, and three *vexillarii*. They were classed according to quality in three ranks of which only the first rank contained the best men. Behind these *triarii* therefore the ranks were called *rorarii*, who threw their *pila* or spears like *dew*, running to the front between the divisions of the *manipuli* and retiring again behind them; others were called *accensi* who were the men on whom least dependence could be placed. In the time of Polybius, the legion was divided differently, the younger troops were called *velites*, or γρόσφοροι, from the spear they carried, their number varying; next came the *hastati*, whose number also varied; and next six hundred *triarii*. But the numbers of these last were never changed. The cavalry remained as before.

The officers were sixty *centuriones* and sixty *optiones* lieutenants chosen by the *centuriones;* the former headed, the latter followed the centuries or *manipuli*. The first chosen of the centurions led the right wing, the second the left. The cavalry were in ten troops or *turmæ*, with three *decuriones* or superior officers and three *optiones* or subalterns to each.

The legion, which had originally consisted of Roman citizens only, gradually included all Romans, and during the last century B.C. all the free population of Italy; under Caracalla the entire Roman world were called upon to serve in their ranks. Allies and auxiliaries were gradually introduced under the name of *socii* who served under their own leaders, *præfecti sociorum*, and encamped apart. In the third century A.D. Goths and others formed entire legions. Down to the end of the republic the legions, though formed and sworn in, were sent after the end of a campaign to their several homes on long furlough, though liable to

serve. But after the time of Cæsar standing armies were
kept up and the military career became a profession, and out
of the pay or plunder acquired by the soldier money could
be saved, or he would receive grants of border land, and was
often settled advantageously in the military stations and
colonies established for the protection of the frontier.

With the introduction of allies or auxiliary forces other
changes had grown in the legion. The entire force was
divided into ten cohorts. The cohorts were still divided
into *manipuli* commanded by centurions, and the whole
body arranged in two lines of five cohorts each. The old
distinction between *velites, hastati, principes* and *Triarii*
ceased. The men were distinguished as those of *levis
armatura* and *gravis armatura.* The various *socii* or
auxiliaries taken into the Roman service were employed as
separate arms of the service, such as Balearic *funditores*
(slingers), Cretan archers, Moorish *jaculatores* (throwers of
darts). Under the emperors the actual legion was supposed
therefore to contain ten cohorts of six centuries of eighty
men each. But the first cohort had the charge of the eagle
and contained double the numbers of the others, viz., 960
instead of 480 men : in all 5,280 men. The old system of
tactics in which the youngest and least experienced men
led the column in order of battle was reversed. The old
soldiers now formed the front line. On the march the
Romans and allies were kept distinct. Each formed their
own advanced and rear guards, and the baggage of each
cohort was carefully guarded, and experienced men, *exploratores*, were sent on to search the country carefully and
save the army from any chances of ambush or surprise.
This seems to have been one of the great uses of the
cavalry, of which the numbers, that is of actual Romans,
were small at all times. They are seen frequently on the
column sent forward to feel for the enemy in the woods
and mountain passes, and are sometimes represented carrying back exact information to the emperor of the progress of a battle actually going on in his front. Besides
these the emperors, like the consuls before them in the days
of the Republic, were surrounded by a select body of men
both mounted and on foot who formed a staff as well as
a body guard, *selecti equites* and *selecti pedites*, each legion
furnished, according to Josephus, 120 horse.[18] The higher

[18] *Principilares, Equites singulares Imperatoris.* These were picked men.
Five horses are seen constantly on the column in attendance on the emperor,
with the same number of attendant officers. *Speculatores* were aides employed
as courriers, or galopers ; *Exploratores* were trained scouts employed to,
ride forward and reconnoitre.

officers, of whom there were six in each legion, were the
tribunes. They commanded about 1,000 men, if the legion
be taken as in round numbers 6,000. When the consuls
were at the head of their constitutional forces, that is
two legions each, they had 12 tribunes under them, and
that was considered to be the regular number in a Roman
camp.

There remains another force to be noted here because a
portion of it was employed and did good service in these
wars,—the Prætorians. Of these Trajan took ten cohorts
or some 10,000 men. These troops were first raised and
formed into a separate corps by the emperor Augustus.
The men were selected, like the French imperial guard,
from the best and most trustworthy soldiers of every legion,
and were a *corps d'élite,* not raised like our own Guards
in the same way as other bodies of the service, which
therefore are not drained of choice men in the process.
A Prætorian cohort, or body guard, had been raised by
Scipio Africanus as a body to attend on the person
of the commander ; but Augustus deemed that something more than this was wanted for the security of
his throne. He wanted an army permanently embodied,
always in full training, equipped and provided, and ready
at a moment's notice for any emergency. This force consisted of nine or ten cohorts, containing a thousand men
each, horse and foot, and of these the politic emperor
stationed only three cohorts in Rome itself, keeping the
others dispersed in different parts of Italy. Tiberius first
assembled the whole force together, summoned them to
Rome and established them in the fortified quarters built
for them by Sejanus, of which the ruins still remain outside
the old wall of Servius Tullius. These quarters contained
permanent buildings, some of them richly decorated, and
of which remains can be traced at the present time. The
camp was dismantled by the Emperor Constantine.

The Prætorians were better paid, or had larger shares of
corn and food, than the ordinary legionaries. Their arms
and accoutrements were richer. Some emperors, such as
Alexander Severus, as a matter of state policy tried to turn
the sentiment of their guards in this direction, that the gold
la vished upon them might be devoted to the splendour of
their horses, armour, and appointments, in which their
military pride might be centred and gratified. It became
a necessity for the successors of Augustus at various
periods to propitiate the Prætorians, who had become
the only source of executive power during the revolu-

tions of the empire. Enormous sums were thus sacrificed at the accession of candidates for the throne of
the Cæsars. But these troops in the reign of Septimius
Severus had to be entirely renewed. He banished the old
Prætorians who had basely deserted the imperial cause
and violated the sanctity of the throne by the murder of
Pertinax, and formed a new guard by selected draughts of
the best soldiers from the various legions stationed on the
frontiers. During the wars of Trajan, illustrated by the
column, the Prætorians had not reached this dangerous or
corrupt condition ; they were still the flower of the Roman
troops.

ROMAN ARMS AND ACCOUTREMENTS.

The arms and accoutrements of the Romans are amply
illustrated in these bas-reliefs. Though the distinctions of
name and arrangements of the ranks and tactics of the
legion had changed, probably the armour and arms of the
soldiers were little altered.

Fig. 3. Lorica lintea. The linen corslet.
From the base of the column.

The light troops performed the part of skirmishers.
Of the *hastati*, half or two-thirds wore cuirasses, the
others wore a cuirass of linen stiffly woven. For this a
frock of mail was sometimes substituted. It reached the
loins. It is not always easy to decide from the bas-reliefs

of what material these frocks were made. In the full-
sized bas-reliefs of the stylobate the chain work can be
made out, and in some of the bas-reliefs of the arch of
Trajan, now on the arch of Constantine, to which they
were removed by the latter emperor, frocks of large and
heavy links are sculptured. All the cavalry and some of
the infantry of Trajan are clothed in a cuirass or mail

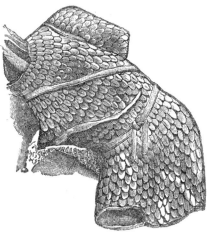

Fig. 4.   Lorica, composed of small plates.
From the base of the column.

coat with short sleeves, and with short linen tunics under.
The artist, in many instances, makes out the chief lines
and forms of muscles under this covering as if it were
extremely tight, and clung to the form like linen or woollen
cloth. In some of these instances embossed leather (cuir-
boulli) is the material represented. The bottom of this
short dress is generally notched. Fine chain mail was
common enough in Rome, and was worn in the armies of
many of the foreign tributaries, as well as in those of the
enemies of Trajan. The use of this protection depended
on the means of the individual officer. Those whose fortune exceeded 100,000 *asses* were expected . to wear chain
mail.

The use of the linen corslet was, however, advocated in
the legions by the military emperor. It had been known
to the Greeks in very ancient times. Herodotus alludes to
such a garment, " θώρηκα λίνεον ἀξιοθέητον ; " and again to
another taken by the Samians, " λίνεον καὶ ξώων ἐνυφασμέ-
νων συχνῶν, κεκοσμημένον δὲ χρυσῷ καὶ εἰρίοισι ἀπὸ ξύλου,'

an admirable corslet richly embroidered with figures of animals, with decorations of gold and tree wool (silk, or cotton?).

Herodotus further remarks, " τῶν δὲ εἵνεκα θαυμάσαι ἄξιον ἁρπεδόνη ἑκάστη τοῦ θώρηκος ποιέει · ἐοῦσα γὰρ λεπτὴ, ἔχει ἁρπεδόνας ἐν ἑαυτῇ τριηκοσίας καὶ ἑξήκοντα πάσας φανεράς."[19] A light garment, every thread of the warp of which contains three hundred and sixty fibres (or fine threads), each clearly discernible. Pliny also speaks of this fact.[20] There is some doubt as to the weaving of these corslets, viz., whether their powers of resistance were owing to the tight plaits or folds into which the garment was sewn together, or to their being glued or mashed together in three or four thicknesses, or to the compactness of the threads of which the material was woven, and both the character of the sculpture on the column, and the old accounts just quoted, favour the latter idea. Galba is said to have put on one of these defences on the day of his death on account of the warnings he had received of impending danger. " *Loricam* tamen induit *linteam*," (to avoid suspicion, for chain mail was also in use), though he could not disguise from himself how little it would protect him from a stab, " quanquam haud dissimulans parum adversus *mucrones* profuturam."[21] It was of use for general wear, as was the buff coat of the seventeenth century, being neither too hot nor too heavy for the most active movements in the field. There were many of these corslets seen by Pausanias in various temples in Attica. He says of them, " Θώρακας δὲ λινοῦς ἰδεῖν ἐν τε ἄλλοις ἱεροῖς ἐστιν ἀνακειμένους καὶ ἐν Γρυναίῳ,"[22] and describing their qualities as compared with those used by the Sarmatians, which were made of slices of horse-hoof sewn together with sinews, he says, " Θώρακες δὲ οἵ λινοῖ μαχομένοις μὲν οὐχ ὁμοίως εἰσὶ χρήσιμοι · διϊᾶσι γὰρ καὶ βιαζόμενοι τὸν σίδηρον, θηρεύοντας δὲ ὠφελοῦσιν, ἐναποκλῶνται γὰρ σφίσι καὶ λεόντων ὀδόντες καὶ παρδάλεων."[23] They are not so often used for fighting, because a bold thrust with the point will go through them; but for sportsmen they do well, for they blunt the teeth even of lions and leopards. The substitution of so useful a defence for the heavy panoply of the metal armour was advocated by the emperors for the reasons already given.

---

[19] Herod. ii. 182 ; iii. 47.   [21] Suet. Galba, xix.
[20] Hist. Nat. xix. 2.   [22] περιηγήσις, Α. κα.
[23] Ælian, Hisp. A. ix. 17.   J. B. Crophu, Ant. Maced. Gronov. VI., 2918. Nepos in Iphicr. Ferrarius de re vest. 2. civ.

The heavily armed men wore the *Cataphracta* (coat of mail) in the time of Vegetius. In the sculptures of the column these heavy troops wear plate armour, and the Prætorians frocks of chain, some coarser in texture than others. Other troops wear *plumata* or feathered armour made of plates sewn on leather, one over the other, like the feathers of birds. The Sarmatians wore armour made of horn, as Pausanias tells in the passage already referred to.

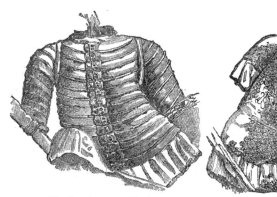

Fig. 5.   Armour of leather.   Fig. 6.   Chain mail.
From the base of the column.   From the base of the column.

The defensive armour in use with the heavy troops of Trajan is in the form of the first kind. A heart preserver nine inches wide was provided to cover the breast, and this was connected by shoulder pieces with a plate of similar kind on the back. From below these, protecting the ribs and reaching to the waist, was a series of plates five or six in number, which were riveted together where the ends met down the middle of the body in front and of the back, and by one or more loose attachments on the sides. They were fastened on leather and secured by a girdle of leather straps round the middle. These pieces lap over or slip under like the shell of the lobster, and as the light armour over the thighs that was in use in this country during the reigns of the Stuart sovereigns, the leather underneath keeping them connected. The shoulders were covered with four or five similar plates which moved up and contracted when required by the movement of the arms at the shoulder joint. The arms were undefended except by the shoulder pieces described. All ranks wore a heavy *galea* or helmet made of four pieces joined by raised ribs which were a further protection to the head. Those of more costly description were beaten out and joined by hammering ; a projecting plate protected the forehead and shaded the eyes, and two jointed cheek pieces flapped down to protect the ears and the sides of the face. In the helmets of officers were worn three or more feathers, high enough to be distinguishable by their men over the heads of the combatants ; sometimes pieces of the skins of wolves. A whole corps or cohort, probably of Prætorians, are sometimes shewn, wearing plumes of feathers. Standard bearers, *signiferi, vexilliferi,* &c., wore over the helmet a complete skin of a bear, lion, or other beast, generally a bear. This was to make them more distinguishable by the soldiers, and more formidable to the enemy. The light troops carried a round or oval shield three feet long of wood covered with hide, with a central boss and a rim of iron, such as may be seen amongst the iron work in the Gibb's collection in the Museum. Some of the *socii,* Gauls and Britons, &c., had shields covered with thin bronze ornamented with a raised rib of admirable wrought work, and further decorated with coral, all hammered up, engraved and set with the elegance of Etruscan workmanship. Two such shields are now in the British Museum, one having been purchased from the Meyrick collection and given by Mr. A. W. Franks, who has fully described them in a learned paper in the Horæ Feriales. The shields of the *gravis armatura* were oblong, made of two boards covered with canvas and calf skin, with a rim and boss of iron, square at the ends, the sides curved inwards ; strong enough to resist great pressure when on the ground. The shields would fit together, and in that arrangement formed the *testudo,* an impenetrable roof. This shield measured 4 feet by 2 and was sometimes a palm longer, protected by light plates above and below the boss. (See further, p. 24.) They wore a linen tunic, linen drawers reaching halfway down the calf of the leg, and sandals. A *focale* or neckkerchief is very general in the column, showing that much of the campaign was carried on through severe weather. They are covered with the *pallium* or short military cloak, nearly square but made with wings or pointed prolongations on two sides. This is buckled or looped by a *fibula* over the right shoulder, but sometimes under the chin in front in very cold weather, or when the men were not required to handle their arms. It is fringed and sometimes notched.

The arms of the legionaries were, in the time of Polybius, two darts, of which the shaft was two cubits or three feet long, the iron equal in length and very carefully joined to

the wood. The head was long, and beaten out to a point
so fine and soft that when thrown it would bend and would
be useless in the hands of the enemy. The shaft was a
finger (perhaps an inch) thick. Several are sculptured on
the stylobate. It is, however, not clear how many of these
darts the light troops used in the time of Trajan. In the
sculptures they never carry more than one.[24] In the days
of the republic they probably carried as many as they
could conveniently hold, and spare arms must have been
carried with the baggage of the legion. In the time of
Vegetius they carried two. " *Triarii cum scutis, cata-
phractis, galeis, ocreati*" (they do not wear greaves on
the column) " *cum gladiis, semispathis plumbatis et binis
missilibus.*" The body guards carried a lance, *hasta*, the
staff four cubits in length, the point barbed, beaten out

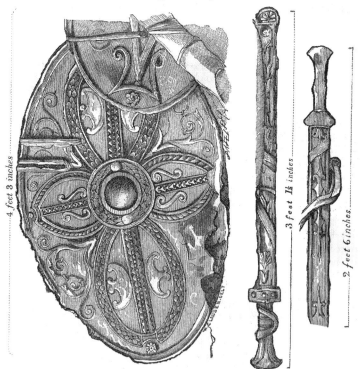

Fig. 7. Arms from the base of the column.

like those of the javelins and bound to the staff by leather
thongs. The heavy troops wore mail, helmets and greaves,

---

[24] Every legion had also darts so hard as to be able to penetrate any armour
or shield—" quibus nullæ loricæ, nulla scuta possunt sufferre." Veget. ii 25.

carried shields, a long and a short broadsword leaded, and two missiles. The rest of the legion carried the *pilum*, a heavy spear, round or square in the staff, with a triangular head nine inches long.

The men carried two swords, one μάχαιρα, was, according to Polybius, Spanish, was worn on the right side, had two edges and a strong point, ὀβελίσκος, like the top of an obelisk. It was a strong dirk or dagger, and very sharp. They had also a longer sword, *gladius* or *spatha*. In the sculptures no instance occurs of two swords being worn, nor is it ever longer than a dagger, but swords of both sizes are shown in the trophies in the more carefully detailed representations on stylobate. The soldiers were trained to strike not *cæsim* but give point, *punctim*, but they appear in the bas-reliefs in most cases to cut rather than thrust. The right foot was advanced in the sword exercise and at close quarters, the left when the spear was levelled to give or withstand a general charge.[25] The *pilum* is the weapon used in most of the combats sculptured, and when they came to very close quarters they used the short dirk as a broadsword, the spear having been thrown and abandoned.

The only officers distinguished by their dress were the tribunes. Trajan is generally seen closely attended by two officers dressed like himself, perhaps Lucius Quietus and the prefect of the Prætorians. They wear bronze cuirasses fitting before and behind, and made to represent the muscles of the chest and body, reaching to the waist, where they meet a skirt composed of strips of leather perhaps covered on the upper end by light plates of bronze. These are girt round the waist, and a portion falls over the girdle, showing the two ends of each thong in a double row of flaps. A rich belt is fastened with a knot round the waist over these thongs, and supports the sword in its usual place on the left hip. The hilt of that of Trajan was of gold and jewelled. It is short and in a thick metal scabbard. When on horseback, and at the galop, he holds it by the scabbard in his left hand. During his speeches and the reception of envoys, he holds the hilt in his left hand. His two officers are in armour like himself. They never carry shields or wear helmets. Trajan is once or twice seen with a lance in his hand.

The common soldiers of whatever rank carried great burdens on the march. Sometimes a cohort or force was detached and marched light, leaving its baggage with the

---

[25] Veget. ii. 16, l. xii., &c., and Tacitus Ann. 12. c. 35.

legion, but only for special services. Usually a Roman private carried something like 60 pounds avoirdupois, about the weight carried into action by the German soldiers from the time of Frederick the Great, and of our own till recent times, and of the French.[26] Josephus pitied the private soldiers as being beasts of burden. Besides his arms and armour the soldier carried provisions, sometimes as much as for 17 days. What the provisions were in Trajan's time it is not easy to specify, *buccellatura*, *laridum* bacon or lard, *caro vervecina*, weather mutton, were amongst the *annonæ*, necessaries or allowances, for which regulations were made in the Theodosian Code '*de erogatione militaris annonæ.*'[27]

The soldier carried his kit on his back, or rather slung

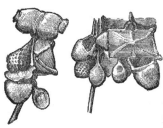

over his shoulder on a stake or *hasta*. It consisted, as in the accompanying woodcut, of, 1, a bag or knapsack, presumably the size of our own, made with straps, crossing diagonally from corner to corner. 2. A small goatskin of wine or vinegar. 3. A pot of metal, with long upright handle. 4. A ladle.

Fig. 8. Soldier's Kit.

5. A net to hold fresh provisions.

Every man was supposed to carry on a campaign besides these things, a saw, πρίονα, basket, κόφινον, mattock, ἄμην, hatchet, πέλεκυν, strap, hook and chain, ἱμαντα και δρέπανον και ἄλυσιν; but, though used frequently along with other tools in the course of the warlike operations in Dacia, they are not shown in the bas-reliefs to have been carried by the men. It should be observed that working parties put their helmets off, plant their spears in the ground, set the helmet on the butt and rest the shield against it, but continue to wear their plate armour, which must therefore have been too light to be any impediment to the use of the arms. They wear their side arms, to part with which in the presence of the enemy, even when the working parties are protected by guards (which is the invariable rule) was a military crime punishable with death. Vegetius adds, that every trade was represented in the legion, as we have already had occasion to notice.[28]

---

[26] E. Guhl und W. Kohner, Das Leben der Gr. und Römer, &c. 7–37.

[27] R. Herm. Schelii notæ in Polyb. Græv. x. 1220.

[28] "Habet præterea legio fabros lignarios, instructores carpentarios, ferra-"rios, pictores reliquosque," lib. i. Carpenters, master carriage builders, smiths, painters, &c.

From the time of Augustus *classici,* or sailors or men of the fighting marine, were attached to the legion. They did not form ' naval brigades,' as has been the case in the English army more than once in late wars, but were employed solely to build and navigate boats, and undertake the duties of the pontoon train in making bridges of boats, &c. Vegetius speaks of something like a complete train of this description, " Scaphas de singulis trabibus (light buoyant canoes) excavatas, cum longissimis funibus et interdum ferreis catenis quatenus contextis eisdem monoxylis supertectis etiam et tabulatis," to serve to make bridges of boats.[29]

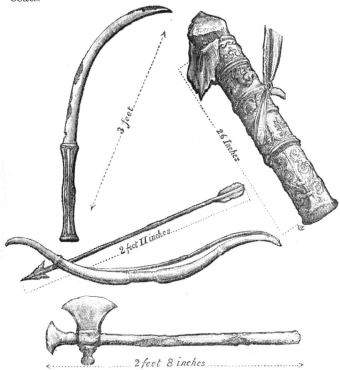

Fig. 9. Arms.

With regard to auxiliary troops, the Germans are, in these sculptures, nude to the waist, and wear loose drawers or trowsers. They fight with clubs, but are always fur-

---

[29] Lib. ii.

nished with shields of Roman make, so that it is probable
that these forces were engaged as tribes or clans under
known heads, and that no time had ever been devoted to
train them for the Roman service, if even such a training
was considered safe or desirable in a population that could
not be permanently kept with the Roman standards.

Slingers are seen in No. LXXXVIII. and in other instances,
who are completely clothed in the tunic and *sagum*, or cloak,
distinctive of the Dacians and their allies, but without the
trowsers, and these were probably borderers engaged in the
course of the war, for they do not appear in the earlier
sculptures. To these must be added archers, dressed in
cuirasses or mail shirts, and long linen skirts reaching to
the ground; Mauritanian horsemen, whose horses are seen,
as in No. XLVII., without saddle or bridle.

I should not pass over, in taking account of baggage,
the luxury which crept into the Roman army, at least
amongst the officers and knights of wealth. We have
in the Museum a curious collection of casts of the camp
service of plate found lately at Hildesheim in Germany,
which had belonged to a Roman general, judging by the
fineness of the work and the general excellence of the
designs; they may probably be attributed to the Romans
of the second century. Mallius, Boccius, and Marsius,
are names of artists found on some of the pieces, which are
upwards of fifty in number. They consist of a large
vessel for holding snow to cool wine, with delicate vine-
leafwork on the bowl; drinking *pateræ*, flat dishes, in
one of which is a noble seated figure of Victory or Minerva,
draped and armed, in full relief, and parcel gilt; another
has a head of an infant Bacchus. There are oblong
silver dishes; cups with and without handles, saucepans,
dishes, a steel-yard for weighing meat in the shape of
a tall terminal figure, and various utensils for the table
and kitchen, some in fragments only. It has been but
a portion of the travelling canteen of the owner. This
splendour was not confined to the general or tribunes.
In giving details of Roman furniture[30] reference has been
made to Pliny the elder, which I may repeat here.
Pompeius Paulinus, a man of equestrian rank at Arles in
Gaul, had to Pliny's own personal knowledge, a service of
silver plate which *he carried with his military baggage on
a campaign*, weighing 12,000 lbs.[31]

---

[30] Woodwork and Furniture : Introduction.
[31] H. N. xxxiii. 50.

Trajan himself was exceptionally simple and unpretending in many ways, but he was given to the pleasures of the table and drank heavily, and the costly and carefully made *papiliones* or tents seem to imply that though he marched bareheaded and on foot, he was not averse to what formed a part of the ordinary state of a commander-in-chief. His tents are made of leather (?), or some rich or warm material. The surfaces are divided (in the sculptures) into squares, and are probably skins of which we see the seams, or perhaps rich materials protected and strengthened by a large network of cordage.

ROMAN STANDARDS.

The standards in the legion were numerous. Every *manipulus* had a *vexillarius* or *vexillifer*, a standard bearer. The ensigns are fully represented in the bas-reliefs. Besides these the cohort had a standard, *draco*, and the legion an *aquila*. These were entrusted to picked men, and were to each subdivision and to the cohort and legion as precious and sacred as the colours of regiments in our modern armies. A careful study of the column will show how great a variety there is between different standards of the first kind. The origin of the standard and of the name *manipulus* seems, according to Ovid, to have been a handful of grass, fern, or other herbage, gathered and tied to the head of the lance.[32] This was replaced by a hand, and hands appear on some of the standards, right, left, open, or with two fingers, or with one finger only open. The hand is on the summit of the spear or shaft. In other standards the top ornament is a small shield, oval, and sometimes it is of other shapes and is surrounded by a wreath. It stands on a short cross bar immediately below the shaft head, and to this bar two narrow strips or thongs are hung, ending in trefoil buttons or ornaments of metal. In some cases small banners, or tablets with pictures on them, surmount the standards. In the composition representing the first passage of a river, there are pictures on the standards, the subjects being images of various divinities. Sometimes there is a small eagle in a wreath, or a plain wreath or a patera. The short cross bar below the top ornament is always seen, even when there is no particular top ornament and the lance's point is shown. Below the cross bar comes a series of round pateras seven or eight in number. In other cases these alternate with busts of emperors, each within a wreath ; in others with an eagle, a mural crown or two, a square plate or round drum, having *rostra* or ships' beaks on each side. Where there are varieties of ornaments of this kind, one below the other, an horizontal torus or block with the edge cut into leaves separates them. Below all is a semi-globe ornamented in the same way, having something of the appearance of a thick short tassel. The round devices were supposed to be significative of the world, and to show the Roman dominion over it. The ancient notion

---

[32] " Portica suspensos portabat longa maniplos
Unde maniplaris nomina miles habet."—Ov. Fastæ, iii.

as to the shape of the earth being that it was a circular plane, not a globe. Other ornamental cross bars occur at intervals on some of the standards. The cohort standard was a piece of cloth fringed with gold, fastened to a cross bar longer than that of the standard just described (below the spear head), which was shown fastened; a dragon was embroidered on this banner, hence called a *draco*. The force under Trajan's command included ten cohorts of Prætorian guards, and these banners where they occur are perhaps those belonging to that body.

The most important of all the standards was the eagle. It was guarded by a double cohort 960 strong. In these sculptures the eagles have sometimes a mural crown over the wings. All the eagles were of bronze; two have been discovered and are now in the Erbach collection. It was of a size small enough to be concealed about the person, and instances are known of the *aquilifer* breaking it off the staff lest it should fall into the hands of the enemy. The top of the pole is fitted with a square bracket moulded with beads in relief and the eagle stands on it. In the opening scene where the army crosses the bridge of boats, there are two eagle bearers *aquiliferi*, but the eagle itself is wanting in one case having been lost under Domitian. This eagle was restored at the conclusion of the war.

The eagle is not the only animal seen on a standard. In No. XXXIV. will be seen a staff and bracket of the same form as those of the *aquilæ* but surmounted by an ' *aries* ' a ram. It was emblematic of siege operations and many sieges were carried out in the course of the first, and more during the second war. Till the time of the second consulship of Marius, B.C. 104, eagles, wolves, minotaurs, horses and boars had been used as insignia of the cohorts. He decided that in future eagles only should be retained and that only one should be taken into action.[33]

---

[33] Michel Angelo Causeo de la Chausse de Signis Mil. ap. Græv. x. 1529. I do not know of the existence of a legion eagle. Those mentioned are small, and belong to standards of cohorts or *manipuli*.

MUSICAL INSTRUMENTS.

It is right before discussing the march and encampments to describe the instruments of military music in use in Roman armies. Drums were unknown. Three kinds of brass wind instuments were in use. The *tuba* was a straight trumpet. The *cornu* was a long curved horn describing more than half of a circle, and connected by an ornamental bar to preserve it from the risk of being bent or broken. The *buccina* or *lituus* was a long horn, straight, but with a curved end. The sounds of the calls given on these instruments differed, and the signals intended could be distinguished accordingly. The day and night were each divided into four watches *vigiliæ*, measured by the *clepsydra* or water clock. The *tuba* called the watches on and the *cornu* called them off. The *buccina* gave the signals for pitching and striking tents, loading the baggage, &c. The *tuba* and *buccina* sounded together for signals for going into action. It is these two instruments that are seen in most frequent use in the various warlike operations sculptured. In the time of Polybius there were three signals on striking the camp. At the sound of the first the tents were struck, beginning with those in the Prætorian or general staff quarters, in which were the tents of the emperor or consul and of the tribunes: at the second all baggage not borne on men's shoulders was loaded on the carts or sumpter beasts of the military train: and at the third the whole army marched. Woodcuts of these details will be seen further on.

CAMPS.

Perhaps few matters of Roman antiquity have been gone into with such prolixity as the form of the Roman encampment. There are materials for ample discussion on the subject, and the reader will see the subject carefully explained in the admirable article on this subject in Dr. Smith's dictionary of antiquities. The usual form was rectangular and the positions of the Prætorian quarters, of the infantry, of the cavalry, pioneers, reconnoiterers, &c., were a matter of strict regulation. Indeed the regulations of Rome on the subject as contrasted with numerous antique earthworks, known in various parts of Great Britain and the continent, have perplexed antiquaries time out of mind, and persons less pedantic and better instructed than Mr. Jonathan Oldbuck.[34] In the sculptures on the Column no military operation is more frequently represented than the entrenched camps made by the Roman army. They are rarely square. Though the representations are never more than conventional or show more than a small structure, sufficient to convey the artist's meaning clearly, yet pains seem to be taken to show that they are round, semi-circular, or irregular in various ways, as often if not oftener than square or rectangular. Indeed though much of the advance must have been carried along the alluvial plains on either side of the Morava, the Tisia, the Theiss, and the Maros, the 'European Pampas' on which to this day flocks of countless sheep are pastured, yet the sculptures most interesting in the history of the war are represented on its uneven theatre, that is in the passes from the bridge of Trajan up to the Iron Gate, about the slopes and forests of the Rothenthurm and other mountainous regions, to which the Dacians retired before Trajan, for they never fought him in the open. It was, therefore, a matter of necessity to encamp on the best piece of ground that could be found.

It is noticeable that the fortified camps on the Column are represented as actual fortresses built of masonry. Into the structure of these military stations we shall enter presently. It is only necessary to call attention here to the fact that clearings made for camps in the forest or among the hills had in view the foundation of permanent stations, and the masonry, &c. shown in the sculptures, refer to the future in many instances, and could only have been

---

[34] Antiquary, i. 50.

founded or begun during the advance into Dacia. But in any case the sites of camps were such as would be useful for forts, having streams sometimes carefully shown, precipitous rocks and other defensive features on one or more of their sides.   Vegetius expressly says that camps must be of any shape that convenience may dictate.   Though that author is inexact in many particulars, he is only telling us here what certainly was, and had been for many years, the custom with Roman armies.

*THE ARTILLERY AND SIEGE TRAINS OF THE TRAJAN
COLUMN.*

Fig. 10. *Dacian Balista.* Mounted as a wall piece.

One of the most interesting features in the sculptures of
the Trajan Column is the representation, difficult to meet
with elsewhere, of the artillery of the Romans.

The Romans well understood the advantage, not only
of being able to inflict loss on an enemy at long ranges,
while he was too distant to annoy their own troops, but
also of the moral weight which the possession of mechanical
contrivances for this purpose would give them.   Some
advantage was gained by the Carthaginians when they
brought elephants into battle.   Besides being formidable
in the actual shock of battle, those monsters inspired
terror from their size, their supposed ferocity, and the
prevailing ignorance about them.   In more ancient times
the weight, size, and space of ground covered by ranks of
armed chariots, in the Asiatic and Greek armies, the mere
noise produced by these vehicles, the jolting and rattle, the
roar of a thousand wheels (without springs) rolling over
rough ground, probably contributed to demoralize an enemy
before any actual contact with the rank or phalanx of
spearmen.[35]   The Romans however did not employ chariots,
and the strength of their army was the infantry.   But as
they had to encounter troops of every nationality, often out-
numbering their own, they carefully developed the inventions of the Greeks for projecting darts, arrows, and stones.

It is not easy to trace the first invention or adoption of
mechanical contrivances for throwing to a distance projectiles heavier or more destructive than could be cast by the
immemorial bow or by slings.   Both those methods of
striking at a distance were in use by the Greeks and by
the older Asiatic nations, including the Jews.   There have

[35] We have lived to hear of a discussion on the re-introduction of *chariots*
into modern warfare.   The use of *cars* to carry riflemen rapidly from one
point to another during action was in this year, 1873, under discussion amongst
military authorities at the United Service Institution.

been at all times also races famous for their skilful training in this respect, and probably gifted with quickness, brightness of sight, and other bodily advantages that fitted certain families or tribes for archery or slinging better than their contemporaries. Thus the city of Gebar, in Judæa, numbered 700 left-handed men who were slingers of such skill that they could strike a hair and not miss,[36] a perfection probably not surpassed by the slingers of the Balearic islands, the Numidian archers of Diocletian, or the famous English yeomen of the middle ages. All these arms are seen in activity on the Trajan column.

I cannot gather from early records when mechanical forces were first employed to project heavy missiles. Yet in siege operations engines of some sort were no doubt employed from a remote antiquity. "There was a small city, with few men within it, and there came a great king against it, and beleaguered it, and built great bulwarks against it. And there was found in it a poor wise man and *he by his wisdom delivered the city.*"[37] This seems to imply an unusual appliance of mechanical skill. In the third century B.C., Archimedes invented and developed warlike engines of various kinds, which were made for Hiero, and were used at a later period in the defence of Syracuse against Marcellus. Whether his levers could actually lift any Roman vessels of war, other than light row galleys, or his burning glasses could set fire to them, according to the tradition, may be questioned; but his inventions in the way of artillery for projecting weights, darts, and combustibles were probably of efficacy sufficient to keep the whole Roman fleet at a safe distance, and turn the siege of the place into a blockade.

Ctesibius of Alexandria, who lived during the third century B.C. taught mathematics and military engineering, and founded a school, or instructed pupils, amongst whom was Heron, at Alexandria. In the Island of Rhodes these sciences were understood and taught, and the Romans got their knowledge from these various schools.

In the time of Cæsar, and probably for two centuries before, the Romans seem to have developed the power of this arm of their military establishments as far as the propelling forces at their command would allow. Probably Greek engineers continued to be the designers of the best and most effective of Roman engines. Various engines are seen on the Column, both in the form of moveable artillery and in other contrivances for the attack of walled towns, which

---

[36] Judges, xx. 16.   [37] Ecclesiastes, ix. 14.

may be termed the field artillery and siege train of Trajan. The field artillery or movable engines followed the march, and amongst the legionaries were engineers, artisans, and workmen, as well as a number of trained artillerymen competent to move and serve their various pieces. They had also amongst the engineers men able, as we shall see in the course of these sculptures, to construct bridges, as well as architects prepared to give plans and superintend the execution of fora, baths, theatres, amphitheatres, &c. in the military stations, which were made permanent, fortified, and provided with these resorts of business, pleasure, or convenience as soon as possible after their occupation as fortified camps.

A book called *Mathematici Veteres* containing several treatises on the siege operations of the ancients, including the construction of warlike engines, was published by Thevenot Boivin and Lahire in the reign of Louis XIV.[38] This book has become very scarce, and the authors whose treatises it contained have been re-edited by M. Wescher.[39] The work contains a treatise by Heron of Alexandria, pupil of Ctesibius, on the smaller engines, χειροβαλλίστρων κατασκευὴ καὶ συμμετρία. Heron wrote about the middle of the third century, B.C. He was the inventor of certain kinds of fountains, and of the application of steam as a motive power. It is said that engines on his plan are still in use in Edinburgh and other parts of Scotland.[40]

2. A treatise by Athenæus, a contemporary of Ctesibius in the second century B.C. He wrote on warlike engines περὶ μηχανημάτα addressed to Marcellus.

3. A treatise on the structure of warlike engines, κατασ-κευαὶ πολεμικῶν ὀργάνων by Biton.

4. Parts of the Πολιορκητικά of Apollodorus, addressed to the emperor Hadrian.

5. Fragments of treatises by Athenæus, Biton, Heron, Apollodorus and Philon of Byzantium, a contemporary of Ctesibius, who treats of the Greek fire, and various methods of attacking walled towns and fortified places.

We may divide the engines described in the treatises, many of which are sculptured on the column, into two classes. 1. Those that were moveable and made for projecting darts or for projecting stones, or those for projecting both stones and darts. These engines were known as *scorpiones, balistæ, catapultæ,* and *onagri,* names which

---

[38] Fol. Paris, 1693.
[39] Poliorcetique des Grecs, par C. Wescher. 8vo. Paris, 1869.
[40] " Nearly the machine afterwards introduced by Avery, one of which of six horse-power is or was at work near Edinborough." Smith's Greek and Roman Biography, &c.

seem to have been used with some confusion, and to have been shifted by different writers from one to another of these machines. Thus in speaking of the distinction used by Vitruvius, Philander his commentator says "nemo " non videt (hoc capite) *catapultis* et *scorpionibus* mitti " *sagittas, balistis* autem jaci *lapides.*" Again he refers to Cæsar, Bell. Gall. ·i. Valerius Maximus i., and Cicero, Tusc. ii., as affirming that *catapultœ* projected stones, and *balistœ* flint balls. Ammianus Marcellinus, b. xxiii., maintains that *scorpiones* projected stones, and *balistœ* arrows.[41] On the other hand, Vegetius, who lived at a later period, declares, l. iv., that the *balistœ* were used for both classes of projectiles. It is, however, to be remembered that the words or names had probably ceased in his time to bear the same exactness of meaning that had originally been intended, and that engines of projection were called by both names.

2. The other division, complicated machines and siege artillery, would include the contrivances of various kinds used in attacking fortified places. The Romans had from an early date certain rough and ready resources for attacking fortified walls. One which was common to all antiquity was the simple resource of piling up a mound of earth equal to the height of the walls, so as to carry the place by storm. Another was the *testudo,* which consisted in the soldiers kneeling, stooping, and standing in close order, and placing their oblong shields edge to edge, so as to form a sloping platform or penthouse, on the top of which other ranks of combatants could climb, and others above them. Above the top rank the men could run up to the parapet as up a mound. This contrivance, however, could only be put in practice when the walls were low, perhaps those of fortified camps, towns hastily walled, and the like. The *testudo* will be seen in action on the column No. XXIII. Rams of various form were also used, some fitted in or over covered sheds, on wheels or rollers, and moveable up to the edge of a fosse, or the base of a wall to be used for battering: *Musculi,* covered sheds to contain machinery such as the *falx,* for boring or mining; towers, platforms, or moveable scaffolds, from which ladders could be laid; ladders with shields on stages contrived to be brought close to the besieged walls; methods of hoisting and lowering swinging bridges and boxes filled with armed men on the walls; methods of projecting fire and combustibles: and platforms and moveable bridges adapted to the decks of ships or boats.

If the later emperors were weak as generals or handled degenerate armies, they had at least the experience of twelve

---

[41] Notæ in Vitruv. lib., x. 15.

centuries in the art of war to guide them, and had profited by every successive mechanical warlike invention of their predecessors. I shall attempt no more than a brief description of such engines as are represented on the column, and of such methods of fortifying walled *oppida* and engineering works as may there be studied, illustrated by reference to Vitruvius and to some fortifications more completely described in Cæsar. I begin with some account of the—

FIELD ARTILLERY OF THE TIME OF TRAJAN.

The smallest of the projecting engines could be handled by one man. It was called χειροβαλίστρον, and is illustrated by the accompanying figure.

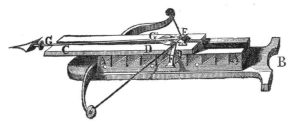

Fig. 11.

This machine is so like the mediæval crossbow that we need not describe it in detail. The motive power is a thick but elastic bow of wood or steel. Into the central beam A, B, a piece of wood C, D, is keyed by a dovetailed tenon, and a small tongue of metal in the upper piece drops into toothings in the lower. This piece is shifted up to the string before it can be drawn back, the tongue and toothing keeping the cord from slipping during the action. The tumbler hook E, cleft in the middle so as to hold the upper end of the dart or arrow G, revolves on a central pin. This hook is kept from revolving by the piece F, which turns on a pin H, (in diagram 12.) When this is pulled back the tumbler is let go, the string released, and the

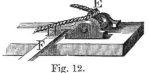

Fig. 12.

arrow projected. It will be noticed that the missile is an arrow with featherings, to keep it steady in its flight; not as was the case with the charge of the mediæval crossbow, a short bolt armed with an iron head.

MOTIVE POWERS OF LARGE ENGINES.

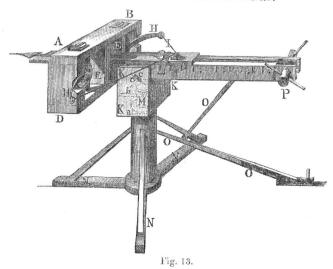

Fig. 13.

The engine, (of which this figure is from Vitruvius,) is of the same nature as the last, but the motive power is different, and it is on a scale large enough to allow it to rank as a piece of artillery, and will be seen frequently sculptured on the column. When required for field artillery, or as a moveable piece to be handled in action and manœuvred about during an engagement, these pieces are seen mounted on wheels. They are set on rectangular platforms, resembling in form the modern London water-cart, and of about the same size. They were called *Carrobalistæ.* The arrows were discharged over the heads of the mules or horses that drew the piece as in No. XXVIII. When on walls or entrench-ments, as in the wooden rampart represented in No. LI., or on the walls of a town, as in the same number, they were mounted on a turntable, supported by a massive column of wood.

The motive power used in these large machines may be illustrated by the accompanying diagrams. A, B, C, D, figure 15, is a frame consisting of thick planks connected by four uprights E, E, A B, D C. The uprights divide this por-tion into three. The side compartments have two round holes (F, F, on plan) bored in the centres of the upper and lower planks. These borings are placed at certain angles with the central parts, as in the annexed plan. Through these holes are passed a number of ropes G, G, made

Fig. 14.

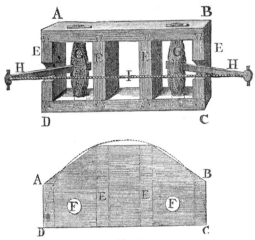

Fig. 15.

of gut, nerves (those of the necks of oxen being preferred), or of women's hair.[42] These ropes were strained by winches till each rope, when struck, was *tuned to the same note*, thence spoken of as τόνοι, tones. They passed through each hole and were secured over a metal pin, somewhat longer than the diameter of the opening; and when the opening was so filled that the last length of the rope passed with difficulty, the end was secured by paying it round with fine cord (as loops are secured in the rigging of ships).

When this mass of ropes was strained in both compartments to an exactly equal degree tested by the sound as above stated, (the rope being stretched to two-thirds of its original thickness,) two arms or levers H, H, were passed through the middle of the two masses of rope. They were drawn inwards and united to each other by a cord.

The whole engine, as seen in the woodcut No. 13, was something like a crossbow or χειρο βαλλίστρον, on a very large scale. The elasticity of the bow is replaced partly by the arms or levers, which were made of elastic wood or of tempered steel, but mostly by the action of the strained ropes C, C.

---

[42] Vegetius, iv. 9, speaks of women's hair as a resource when rope could not be made out of other materials. There seems, however, a concurrence of opinion among both Greek and Latin engineers in favour of this material as the best that could be used, being close, strong, and elastic.

These engines were mounted on turntables formed as is shown in the first figure. K, K, K, in fig. 13, is a strong wooden frame with a thick board at the base *a, a,* and another at *b, b.* L is a solid column of timber with a smaller column M (in dotted lines) at a certain height (about 4 feet). The column rests on three timber feet N, N, N, and the smaller neck M passes through the pieces *a, a,* and *b, b,* so that the frame K, K, K, rests on the shoulder of the larger column, and can be turned in any direction. The machine swings in the upper part of the frame K, K, K, on a metal axle *c,* and is balanced so that it can be elevated or depressed. The jointed rest O, O, O, keeps it at the elevation required, and as this rest is made to shift round the column the piece can be turned, elevated, or depressed in any direction required.

The catapult for hurling stones is made on the same principle, as will be seen on reference to fig. 17. The construction is stronger, and there are screws for tightening the strained cords at *a, a, b, b.* The force required to wind up the string being greater than in the case of the smaller and more handy engines, the pulleys and ropes used for this purpose were made fast to walls, posts, or whatever could be conveniently made to serve as a sufficient fulcrum, not to the beam of the piece itself.

Another kind of engine was called an *onager,* or wild ass.[43] These engines were provided with one set of ropes instead of two, strained horizontally from one side of the whole engine to the other. A single lever twisted into the ropes was drawn back by two winches, worked by two men each, till it had described two-thirds of a semicircle, and fastened by a hook and stay, as the cord of the *balista.* To the end was attached a sling containing a round flint ball. The *magister* when all was ready, struck the small metal stay or trigger a smart blow with a mallet, and the lever being released flew back, hurling the flint ball from the sling in a parabolic flight. The name *scorpio* was sometimes given to an engine of this description.[44] The Greeks in some of their balistas seem to have used actual steel bows, instead of ropes as in the accompanying, taken from the diagram of Biton, in which the sling for stones, shown at A, is in addition to the apparatus for discharging darts.[45]

[43] Ammian. Marcellin. **xxiii.** " Quod asini feri cum venatoribus agitantur " ita eminus lapides post terga calcitrando emittunt ut perforent pectora " sequentium aut perfractis ossibus capita ipsa displodant."
[44] " Quoniam aculeum desuper habet erectum."
[45] Poliorcetique des Grecs, p.   .

The apparatus for hooking and holding the string, holding and releasing the hook, and discharging the projectile, is the same as we have seen used for the smaller engine. The board or bar on which the string moved was drawn down along with the cord and provided with a tongue to catch in the teeth cut in the lower frame. This lower frame is prolonged and made to contain a winch P in fig. 13 that was turned by two or by four men.

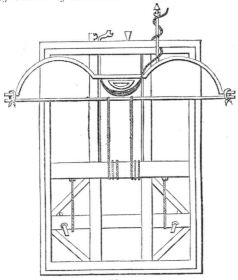

Fig. 16.

In all engines it was of the utmost importance that the string of the *balista* and the lever of the horizontal engine should be protected from the effect of the discharge, the string being liable to strike the fore part of the frame that contained the ropes and the lever to strike the fore framework of the *onager* with still more violence. For this reason these portions were padded with pillows [46] of hair and sacking, and the same was done in the case of the *onager*, the fore part of which was padded either with a thick hair cushion or heaps of turf. The force of the discharge was so great in the latter case, that the parapet of any wall on which it was mounted would be loosened and thrown down by the concussion.[47] In the case of the *balista*, to make the bow of which there were two arms and two sets of tension ropes, it was of the utmost importance that

---

[46] " Pulvileo." Vitr. xc.

[47] "Muro saxeo hujusmodi moles imposita disjectat quicquid invenerit " subter, concussione violente non pondere." Amm. Marcellin., xxiii.

the mass of ropes on each side should be of one tone or
strained to the same pitch (tested in the case of each rope
by the ear), otherwise the force of the discharge would not
be equal in both arms, the momentum of the projectile
would be diminished, and the flight, it was supposed, would
be erratic.

Minute directions are given in Vitruvius, who follows the
Greek engineers, as to the proper method of straining and
fastening the ropes, as also for the proportions of the parts.
The force of the engine to which the length and size of
the projectile were proportioned depended on the size of
the openings through which the ropes passed and where
they were held, the amount of the motive power being
regulated by the larger or smaller number of ropes that
could pass through these holes or bores, and the greater
or less momentum they could impart to the projectiles.
The *bore* was the test of power of the engine.

Catapults for hurling stones were made of all sorts
of calibres, bores, or power. The lightest were made to
throw stones of 2 or 3 pounds in weight, others for
heavier stones, increasing (if Vitruvius is to be believed,)
to 300 and 350 lbs. Much, however, of his descriptions is
to be received with caution.[48]

Not only stones but beams were projected from some of
these engines. Josephus speaks of them as battering down
great masses of masonry, and destroying ranks of men at
single discharges. They could disable a hostile vessel in
action, so as to prevent her making her port, by breaking
her masts, staving in planking, &c.

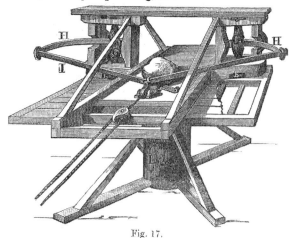

Fig. 17.

[48] Philander, note to Vitruvius, x.

NUMBERS USED IN THE FIELD.

The numbers of engines used in Trajan's time in the field cannot be stated. Vegetius Renatus wrote in the time of Valentinian, and his treatise is drawn from all kinds of authorities. As, however, one source of his information was the imperial decrees of Augustus, Trajan, and Hadrian he is probably to be depended on for the details he gives of the artillery of the two last emperors, and of its condition in his own day. According to this author each *centurio* was provided with one *carrobalista,* and the number of soldiers required to man each piece was eleven. Fifty-five such pieces accompanied the legion. Besides these pieces, ten *onagri* were assigned to the legion, one to every cohort, each being drawn on a carriage by oxen; on the column they are drawn by mules.[49]

---

[49] " Per singulas centurias singulas carrobalistas, item decem onagros hoc est " singuli per singulas cohortes in carpentis bobus portantibus." Veget. iv. 25

Siege Engines.

Mention has already been made of a sort of pontoon train, *Scaphas de singulis trabibus* [50] boats or canoes hollowed out of logs of timber, with long ropes or iron chains, on which planks can be laid and bridges constructed. If such small boats are not seen to have been used by Trajan, the reason probably was because the rivers he crossed were navigated by boats in numbers more than were required for these purposes, and which kept pace with the advance of his expedition.

For siege operations such as are shown on the column, a great variety of mechanical contrivances were in use derived mostly from the Greek engineers, perhaps occasionally improved by Roman artificers. The authors in the Poliorcetique give diagrams of different forms of moveable sheds. Of the battering ram there were several varieties. To some were attached covered sheds and machinery, such as drills to bore the walls, of which the axle was turned by a large bow and cord.

Musculi, Muscles were sheds covered first with boards then in some instances with bricks and mortar, and over these with skins to protect the wet mortar from disintegration by water thrown on it, and over the skins with old cloth rags to preserve the skins from fire. The shed here represented is taken from the Poliorcetique. Cæsar describes such a construction as nine feet long. It was a shed erected on two beams laid parallel to each other four feet apart, supported by short pillars five feet high covered with boards protected by metal plates and fastened with nails of metal, roofed over with brick vaulting as described.[51] *Musculi* were pushed forward on rollers or wheels, and prepared the way for the *turres ambulatoriœ*, moveable towers, of

Fig. 18.

[50] Veget. *ib.*   [51] Bell. Civil. ii. 10.

which the example here given was constructed by Cæsar at Alessia.[52]

Fig. 19.

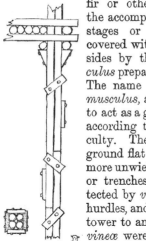

The angles of the *turres ambulatoriæ* were made of fir or other poles nailed together, as in the accompanying from Jules César. The stages or floors were made of timber covered with hurdles and protected at the sides by the same materials. The *Musculus* prepared the ground for these towers. The name was derived from that of the *musculus,* a fish supposed by the ancients to act as a guide to the whale, which animal, according to Pliny,[53] could see with difficulty. These small covered sheds beat the ground flat for the advance of larger and more unwieldy towers. The advanced lines or trenches of besiegers were further protected by *vineæ,* sheds covered with wattle hurdles, and by bridges from one temporary tower to another. According to Vegetius,[54]

Fig. 20. *vineæ* were sixteen feet long, seven broad, and were supported on posts eight feet high. Other forms of sheds were pushed to the foot of the wall and protected the men employed in mining. Of these engineering works several are shown on the column, in the greatest and most important siege by which the last stronghold of Decebalus was taken in the second war. Several seem in that composition to have had their coverings destroyed and to have been abandoned. All the engines in that bas-relief are such as Vegetius called *plutei.*[55] They stand on three wheels, two

---

[52] Jul. Cæsar, Life, by the Emperor Napoleon, plate 32.

[53] "Ut sub ea milites terram solidarent munirentque viam turribus ambula-" toriis dum muros accederent unde nomen ei factum a marinis musculis qui" balænis prænatant et vada demonstrant."—Facciobati.

[54] Lib. iv.   [55] Vegetius, iv. 15.

in front and one under the rear. They are armed with
the *falx*. The *falx* was a strong iron hook curved into
the shape of a sickle ; as soon as a stone had been displaced
by mining, the hook was introduced and the whole weight
of the engine applied to drag the surrounding stones out of
the wall and to form a breach. The *falx* in the engines
alluded to is fixed on the end of the axle of the fore-
wheels. The axles are made to turn, the wheels having
been jammed by means of handspikes or fixed bars which
are shown in the sculpture. What is not shown is a covering shed to protect the men at work. Behind the rear
wheel of the engines described there is a long bar or pole
jointed into the axle, the other end of which passes through
a round cage like the top that surmounted the mast of
mediæval ships. This was hoisted up by ropes round the
windlass already mentioned and could be dropped on the
parapet of the walls, or from it three or four men could
annoy the defenders with arrows.

Platforms or cages to hold armed men were made to
slide up and down between lofty standards planted outside
their four corners, raised by means of chains and pulleys ; or
were contrived to be pushed up one inside another in the
fashion of telescopes ; or were screwed up by one great screw
press under the centre. Some were swung at one end of a
beam which was poised on its middle, so that the frame could
be swung on the parapet of a wall, and withdrawn by
ropes at the other end of the beam. A number of other
ingenious methods of annoying the besieged or undermining
their walls are propounded by the Greek engineers, but as
they do not figure in the operations of Trajan in his Dacian
war, they need not be discussed further. It may also be
reasonably doubted whether amongst these contrivances
there are not some which never went beyond the pages of
mathematical treatises. A ram is represented in No. XXIII.
as worked by the Dacians by hand. It is mounted at the
end of a long piece of timber and hammered by the vigorous
arms of a number of men against the wall of a Roman
stronghold. The figure of a ram, Fig. 21, roofed to protect a
storming party is from the arch of Septimius Severus in
Rome.

There were many constructions adapted to vessels of war,
fitted on the decks of boats and intended to operate against
sea walls and fortifications. But they have no place in these
Trajan sculptures, as the naval operations on the column are
confined to transport services.

It will not be without interest to know that examples of
the *balista* and other engines of Roman warfare have been

made in modern times. The author of the life of 'Jules 'César,' the late Emperor Napoleon the Third, had several *balistœ* constructed besides an *onager*, and helmets, lances, swords, &c. These curious engines and weapons are now in the museum of Roman antiquities at St. Germain-en-Laye. They are of different sizes and degrees of propelling power, are mounted on wheels, and have something of the imposing appearance of ancient pieces of European or Oriental ordnance. The fore frame of the largest is protected by a mantlet of panelled wood elegantly painted after an antique example. These pieces have been tested at the French artillery ranges, and as I have been informed, made good practice at 600 metres with darts 7 or 8 feet long of oak or ash an inch in diameter tipped and feathered with iron. At that distance several boards were pierced and the missiles were crushed up by the force of the impact from these discharges. The smaller engines were found best as regards accuracy of aim. Great care had to be taken to pad the uprights of the forepart of the structure, lest the string on the arms or bow should be wounded from striking after the discharge.[56]

Fig. 21.

These engines continued to be used as long as the Greek empire was in existence and for a long time after the invention of gunpowder and the introduction of cannon.

---

[56] Nor are these mechanical forces so entirely out of date that we may not witness some re-introductions of them in modern warfare. Sir William Palliser has assured me that for the projection of torpedoes some agent less rapid and sudden than gunpowder is absolutely needed, that they may be discharged against a ship's side without too great risk to the vessel or fortification that uses this means of attack or defence. Thus, along with the use of chariots in battle, naval armour, and heavy beaks at the bows of ships of war for ramming, the gradual revolution of time seems to be restoring to us for certain purposes what many would think the clumsiest of substitutes for our

From the eleventh to the close of the fifteenth centurie they were regularly employed in well appointed armies in Europe, and were carried by sea in pieces or sections to the wars of the crusades. The reduction of Jerusalem under Godfrey and the princes engaged with him could not be completed till heavy and costly battering engines of various kinds, as well as moveable towers provided with platforms and swinging bridges had been constructed and moved to the walls. In addition to the machines of Roman shape and form, the Emperor Napoleon the Third had a number of full-sized machines made for the purpose of ascertaining the range and power of those used in the Middle Ages. "The great projecting engines of the Middle Ages were made of wood, of steel, and even of horn, and the bows were sometimes more than 30 feet in length. Colonel Dufour calculates that such a machine could throw an arrow of half a kilogram in weight to a distance of about 860 yards. They were called *espringales,* and were like exaggerated forms of the crossbow." [57]

In the ancient armoury of Soest in Westphalia a number of missiles and portions of engines of the early 15th century are still preserved. A fragment of a projectile measures one inch and a half in diameter, and is feathered with iron. Smaller ones measure 16 inches by half an inch diameter, and are of oak feathered with slips of applewood, *placed so as to give a rotatory flight.*

The bows of some smaller engines are of wood ; others of whalebone about 6 feet to 8 feet in length, arranged in many thicknesses like modern carriage springs.

The *trebuchet* answered in effect to the *onager* of the ancients and was of use for vertical projection. It consisted of a tapering beam pivoted on trunnions and having a heavy weight at the short end. The longer portion had a sling holding a stone attached to it. It was drawn down by windlasses, and at the proper moment suddenly released.

scientific modern artillery. At the same time it is, I believe, the judgment of some authorities on modern artillery that great weights projected at low velocities are more serviceable by racking and detaching armour plates than shot that can pierce them ; but these opinions only have reference to different classes of guns, not to any comparison between the real power of gunpowder and other propelling agencies. "Notwithstanding the great improvements in " modern machinery, it may safely be affirmed that by no application of the " property of elasticity in metallic, wooden, or other springs could a con- " venient machine have been formed to propel a 32 lb. shot at a velocity of " 1,600 feet a second, although it is highly probable that one might have been " constructed to propel *very large masses at a low velocity, or to produce great* " *momenta,* as was indeed the case with some of the projectile machines of " the ancients."—Art. on Artillery. Encyclop. Britannica.

[57] Le passé et l'avenir de l'artillerie," Vol. ii.

The sling was hurled into the air, a ring at one end slipped over the hook by which it was attached to the beam at an angle of about 45°, and the stone shot upwards in a parabolic course.

The accompanying woodcut is from the Emperor Napoleon: ' Passé et l'avenir de l'artillerie.'

Fig. 22.

Stone shot, beams, putrid carcases to poison the air, even the bodies of living prisoners to inspire terror, could be projected by these engines into besieged places. At the siege of Auberoche an emissary was seized and shot into the town "Si que pour eux plus grever ils prirent le varlet et lui pendirent les lettres au cou, et le mirent tout en un mont en la fonde d'un engin et puis le renvoyèrent dedans Auberoche. Le varlet chéi tout mort devant les chevaliers qui là éstoient, et qui furent moult ébahis et deconfortés quand ils le virent."[58] The experiments and calculations of Colonel Dufour show that without the sling, other things remaining the same, the range of these machines would be reduced by *more than a half*. The siege towers and engines were named *chats, chats chastel, beffroy*, and in English *sows*, and other names.

Some of these engines were violently pulled by numbers of men who replaced the action of the dead weight of the counterpoise, as numbers of men now jump from a height

[58] Froissart, cxcvi.

to raise the iron monkeys used in pile driving or in unloading coals and other heavy cargoes on the Thames. " In
some of these engines the counterpoise consisting of a
timber case filled with stones, sand and the like, was permanently fixed to the butt end of the shaft. This seems to
have been the ' *Trebuchet*' proper. In others the counterpoise hung free on a pivot from the yard, while a third
kind combined both arrangements. The first kind shot
most steadily and truly, the second with more force." [58]

The Emperor Napoleon caused a *trebuchet* to be made
with a shaft of 33 ft. 9 in. in length weighted with a permanent counterpoise of 3,300 lbs. and a pivoted counterweight
of 6,600 lbs. in addition. This engine could not carry a
24 kilo. shot beyond 191 yards, and the piece was much
damaged by the concussion of each discharge. It was
found, however, that by increasing the strength and size of
the machine there would be nothing impracticable in projecting at long ranges projectiles of far greater weight.
The authorities quoted by Colonel Yule mention an engine
employed by the Venetians at the siege of Zara that shot
stones into the city of 3,000 lbs. weight. The French experiments proved that these engines could be directed with
surprising accuracy.[59]

An immense amount of timber was sometimes required
for the construction of one engine in the Middle Ages.
One used at the final capture of Acre was loaded in a
hundred carts. Richard Cœur de Lion had one that filled
an entire ship. St. Louis captured 24 on the Nile, the
timber of which sufficed to stockade his entire camp. The
number of engines was still more enormous in some well
appointed mediæval armies, for the siege of Acre it is said
that 92, by some that 300 engines were set in battery.[60]

1 will conclude these notices with a few words on the
fortifications, of which such numerous varieties occur in the
sculptures on the spiral of the column. They are generally
represented as made of hewn masonry, which could not have
been the case with Roman fortified camps, at least during
the progress of a march.

---

[58] Col. Yule, 124.

[59] At the siege of Thun l'Evêque in 1340, six great engines were brought
from Cambray and Douay. Their vertical discharges broke in the roofs of
houses and towers, driving the inhabitants and defenders to the cellars for
safety.

At the siege of Mortagne Saintonge in 1405, an engineer constructed a
machine on the walls to keep down the discharges of one powerful piece in
the besieging lines. At the *third shot* he succeeded in breaking the beam or
shaft of the besieging engine.—Froissart, i. cxx., &c. &c.

[60] See Col. Yule, ii. 120.

SYSTEMS OF FORTIFICATION EMPLOYED BY TRAJAN AND THE DACIANS.

Valla, ramparts, and ditches were commonly made of turf and timber by the Romans, and we shall best illustrate the bas-reliefs representing these fortifications by a reference to the more complete descriptions given of similar works by Julius Cæsar. From the life by the Emperor Napoleon III. I borrow the accompanying illustrations.

In the Bell. Gall., Book IV. is a detailed account of the Roman field works at Alessia. First a fosse was dug 20 feet wide with vertical sides so as to be as wide at the bottom as on the ground level, in order to make this a real protection against night attacks along lines so extensive, and which men could ill be spared to guard along its whole length, and to protect workmen from the missiles of the enemy during the day. 400 feet behind this fosse was the wall or *vallum.* He then dug two fosses 15 feet wide, filling the inner fosse nearest the town with water from the river Oserain. Behind this inner fosse was raised a rampart and palisade, together 12 feet in height. Against this was placed a fence of hurdles with battlements, *loricam pinnasque.* Strong forked branches were laid horizontally at the point of junction of the hurdle fence with the rampart to make them more difficult to scale. Towers were raised with intervals of 80 feet between. Tops or large branches of trees, of which the extremities were sharpened to a point, were planted in a fosse five feet deep, and every three connected together at the bases so as to make it difficult to pull them

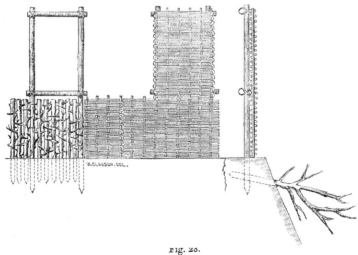

Fig. 26.

up. The branches rose above the ground in the shape of a hedge. Five rows of these were planted contiguous to and interlaced with each other. They were called *cippi*. In front of these were *scrobes*, pitfalls three feet deep, disposed in the form of a quincunx. In the centre of each hole was planted a stake as thick as a man's thigh pointed and hardened in the fire. This stake rose about four feet above the ground. To make it firmer the earth in which it was planted was well rammed down, and the rest of the excavation covered with thorns and brushwood to conceal the trap. They were in eight rows three feet apart and were called *lilia* on account of the resemblance of their form to the bell of that flower.

Lastly in front of these defences were fixed, level with the ground, stakes one foot long armed with iron hooks called *stimuli* placed near each other, all over the space in front. Five have been found in the excavations.

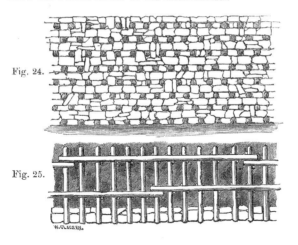

Fig. 24.

Fig. 25.

W. CLAUSEN.

From the Life of Julius Cæsar.—Plate 20.

The Gaulish walls at Avaricum, represented in the accompanying woodcut, were made in the same manner as those seen in No. LVIII. and in No. LXXXVIII., the last and greatest of the strongholds taken in the second Dacian war, as represented on the Column.

The walls in the Gaulish works are partly of earth with layers of timber logs laid at certain heights athwart the thickness of the wall as in the elevation in No. 24. They are held in the wall by longitudinal ties, as in the plan.

The wall is thus faced with stones, and backed with earth, the whole firmly tied together by the timbers inserted at intervals. It would seem as if the same method had been used by the Dacians.

In the walls of the stronghold of Decebalus the walls between the rows of timberwork are faced with irregular masonry, such as is seen on a large scale in the old walls of Alatri, in the Apennines, and in other cities of antiquity, called *cyclopean.* If the stones are large, and if they are well cemented, on whatever scale, the irregularity of the shape does not prevent the construction of a wall of great strength and more difficult of attack by the *falx* or dragging hook of the ancients than if the stones were regularly coursed.

GATES.

The formation of the gates is seen in many of these sculptures. Gateways were recessed or covered by a projecting portion of wall, and then contrived to open in a line parallel, or at right angles with the wall, as in plans A, B, C, D, E, so as to be the more easily defensible from within. These plans are taken from those given in Cæsar's camp on the Aisne, and they answer to the arrangements in many camps sculptured on the Column.

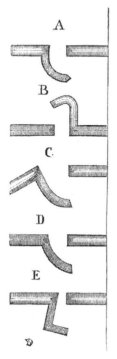

Fig. 26.

They were defended by doors or gates and *clathra* or *fores clathratæ*, portcullises,—*funibus ac catenis ita suspensæ ut demitti et subduci possint, prout re postulat, quales in urbium aut arcium aditu, hostium irruptione propulsandâ in usum remanserunt.*[61] In one of the gates of Pompeii the channels down which such doors were intended to be dropped can still be distinguished. They are frequently seen on the column.

According to Vegetius, the besieged provided themselves with horschair, woollen cloths, etc. to protect the wooden defences from fire. Crates full of stones were placed between the *pinnæ* or battlements.[62] Over the door the wall was to be provided with scuttle holes for pouring water down to extinguish attempts to fire the doors. Platforms for this purpose are frequent on the column. Amongst the stores required by the besieged were bitumen, sulphur, hot pitch, and oil ; iron *utriusque temperaturæ*, hard for weapons, soft for engines, hoop iron, &c., wood, nails, great wheels to let down and set on fire to run amongst the men and horses of the besiegers, timber in proper scantlings for the construction of spare machines. For the same objects, hides and horns, horses' hair, and the long hair of women were kept amongst the warlike stores of strong places, when these were properly provisioned for military operations.

---

[61] Maigne d'Arnis Lexicon med. et inf. Latinitatis, &c. in verb.
[62] Vegetius, iv. 5.

SACRIFICES AND RELIGIOUS RITES.

Few circumstances in the conduct of the Dacian war will strike the student of these sculptures more forcibly than the piety or the religious zeal of Trajan. His careful attention to religious observances was of more importance than the speeches, which the emperor, though a man of Cromwellian simplicity in many respects, was fond of making to his soldiers.

Trajan's religiousness, at least his earnest desire to fulfil all the required rites throughout his campaign, was thoroughly in accordance with the belief of a powerful and sagacious ruler, that the true welfare of the empire and the success of any important enterprise, such as the conquest and annexation of the great Danubian provinces, depended not a little on the careful adherence to good old precedents in religious belief and practice. He neglected no means of a material or military kind likely to be available for securing his victories, but at the same time he seems to have been firmly convinced that much of the chances of war, after every precaution, remains in suspense, and could be inclined to this side or that at the pleasure of the gods.

Trajan also instituted sacrifices after his victories, and rites for the dead, in honour of those who had fallen in the campaign. He is himself in these sculptures the chief agent in the sacrificial rites. This was in his character of Pontifex Maximus. In earlier ages that office was elective.[63] Priests of different worships, such as that of Jupiter, Quirinus, &c. were enrolled in colleges, corporations, or chapters, and filled up vacancies each in their own body. There were besides heads elected to each. The kings in the early years of Rome were sacrificial kings besides, and supreme in matters of worship. Under the republic this union of sacred and political power was dissolved. It had begun with Numa, who kept the chief religious offices in his own house and was present at all important religious sacrifices ; but its hereditary possession then came to an end. The priesthoods were still as before in the hands of great Patrician families, but the high priesthood was transferred to the *Gentes*, who had all along possessed the right of filling up inferior dignities. According to Roman ideas the genuine rites, (and the greatest stress was laid in the exact observance of traditional ceremonies,) were something propagated in *Gentes,* and their comprehension could not be transferred to aliens. Much, too, of the worship was secret, and the possession of secrets so useful

---

[63] Döllinger, Jew and Gentile, B. vii.

to the maintenance of the Roman power would be dangerous in the hands of strangers or enemies. The religious functions hitherto discharged by the kings passed to the *Rex sacrorum*, a sacrificial king created for the purpose. He was excluded from government offices, stripped of political power, and was chosen by the colleges of pontiffs and augurs. He was under the jurisdiction of the *Pontifex Maximus*, though superior to him in his religious character. The *Pontifex Maximus* was the highest authority, and as nothing was done by the State, either in filling up offices, proclaiming war, or making peace without special public religious acts of sacrifice, his power grew to be very great, for everything depended not on the pious intentions of the worshippers, but on the exact administration of the rites, after which the gods invoked were bound to render the help required of them.

Up to the time of Augustus the several colleges remained independant. Cæsar was exalted by the Roman Senate to a seat in the hierarchy of the gods as a descendant of Venus. He was called Jupiter. A temple was decreed to him and *Clementia*[64] on account of his mildness, in which the deities extended their hands to each other. Antony became the *Flamen* of the new Jupiter. He had not, however, a temple dedicated to himself. Augustus during his lifetime would not allow of his own worship, at any rate in Italy. After his death his *apotheosis* took place, and his worship commanded even colleges of worshippers. He took care to add to his imperial dignity, as soon as that was secure, the solid addition of that of *Pontifex Maximus*. It was the keystone of his power, and descended to his imperial successors. All colleges of priests were under them. Augustus filled benefices, nominated the Vestal virgins, decided on the authority of books of augury and soothsaying, interpreted prodigies, always matters of superstitious observance, and consulted and decided on those of the Sybilline books. In all religious cases, and over all causes and persons, and all cases of religious offences he was supreme. The power, too, of the *Pontifex Maximus* hitherto confined to Rome, was now extended over the world. Pliny the younger, accordingly consults Trajan[65] as to the legality of removing an ancient shrine dedicated to the mother of the gods in his government of Bithynia.

It is not necessary in this place to give any detailed account of the vast number of regular and periodical sacrifices re-

---

[64] Döllinger, Gentile and Jew, vii. 1.   [65] Ep. x. 73, 74.

quired by law and custom in Rome itself.   Not only the seasons required that particular gods should receive sacrifices and *lectisternia* (dinners laid out for them with seats covered with rich materials prepared for their use), but at every fresh conquest of a city it was the custom solemnly to invite the gods worshipped in it to desert those abodes and transfer their worship to Rome, where the conqueror undertook to offer them a more complete and sumptuous devotion. In later times, and after the return of Trajan from the Dacian campaigns, processions were prolonged during many days, and the demands of public worship became excessive. It was a ruling idea in the Roman mind that no god should be left out or done injustice to, as there might be no saying when or how he would retaliate such neglect.   It was the business of the *Pontifex* to meet religious emergencies of all sorts.   There was little poetry in the Roman religion, and the position of Greek mythology in the literature of Rome is no measure of any similar hold over the religious thoughts or observances of Romans.   The system of the Roman gods was a most faithful mirror, reflecting every act of public as well as private life with perfect accuracy. Whatever the Roman undertook, a special deity was sure to be at hand ; whatever happened in nature among the beasts, such as good or bad fortune in agriculture, or monstrous births, in vegetable or in human life, a god had done it, and the immediate requirements of public and of private life were the soul and principle of growth of the Roman religious system.   Thus in two or three instances, Nos. XVI., CVIII., we see the interference of divinities to decide difficult actions, or to give to the Romans light by the rising of sun or moon, when fighting in dangerous defiles, where, no doubt, the barbarians might have gained important advantages from ambushes and from their knowledge of the ground.

Once Jupiter interferes with thunder and lightning, perhaps when the Dacians are meant to be represented in overpowering numbers, reminding us of the storms preceding the battles of Crecy, Agincourt, and Waterloo, though Jupiter was not invoked on either of those occasions.

From the date of the laws of the 12 tables, each deity had appropriate animals.   White cattle, with gilded horns, were sacrificed to Jupiter Capitolinus, but no bull or ram.   A bull could only be sacrificed to Apollo, Neptune, or Mars.   Asses, cocks, and horses were also sacrificed to Mars.   Swine to almost all agrarian deities.   To Mars, Ceres, and Tellus, these animals were sacrificed in imprecations and on concluding treaties.   To the gods of the infernal regions black animals were offered with their necks bowed downwards, and their blood was poured into a hole dug on purpose. These various selections of animals, cakes, fruit, &c., are seen in many of Trajan's sacrifices. White cattle, sheep, and swine were the beasts most frequently offered.

Mars had originally been a favourite deity at Rome, and was guardian of flocks and herds as well as god of war, and the sacrifice of lustration or purification offered to Mars was called *Suovetaurilia*, the animals being swine, sheep, and bulls. They were conducted three times round the whole people and sacrificed to Mars. These are the sacrifices most frequently represented on the column. The animals are always sculptured with the utmost fidelity to nature. In these sacrifices, if the entrails did not give favourable signs of the appeasement of the deity, the sacrifice had to be repeated till they did. In Cato [66] the formula given is, "Father Mars, if anything in the previous sacrifice has been not to your mind, so now do I propitiate thee by this new sacrifice." Cæsar after a hundred sacrifices could not, on the day of his assassination, arrive at a favourable appearance of the entrails.

Special attention had to be paid to the choice of victims. The length of the tail was to be considered. No calf was fit, of which the tail did not reach the joint of the leg. In a sheep the tail was not to be pointed, the tongue cloven, nor the ear black.[67] An ox was to be white. If he had spots they must be rubbed with white chalk.[68] It was a bad sign during the sacrifice if the ox bellowed on reaching the altar or after receiving its death wound, or ran away. The *popæ* or *victimarii* are seen in these sculptures with an axe or mace intended to stun the animal at the first blow, so as to avoid the danger of such accidents. The fillets, bands, or stole, with which it was tied, had to be taken off at the altar, and the *popa* held it by one of its horns, as anything fastened to it was of bad import. So also it was unfavourable if the animal did not bleed copiously or sprinkled its blood on the assistants, or did not fall in the right position, or if the portions to be burnt burnt ill, or the flames did not ascend straight up to heaven.

[66] De Re. R. 1141. [67] Plin. H. N. viii. 70. [68] Juvenal, X. 66.

SACRIFICIAL CEREMONIAL SHOWN ON THE COLUMN.

The pontiff veiled himself in the *Cinctus Gabinus,* that is with the *toga* drawn over the head after the fashion of Gabii : and after bathing in spring water, washing his hands clean, was dressed entirely in white so as to be externally pure. The toga and even the shoes were white. The animal had a libation of wine or water poured upon its head, and was qualified if it moved or trembled during this action. *Far* (meal) and salt were sprinkled on each victim, on the sacrificial knives, and on the altar. Next the pontiff cut off hair from the forehead of the victim as a consecration of the whole animal, and this bunch of hair, with incense and a libation of wine, was thrown into the fire, as will be seen in the sacrifices so often represented during the second Dacian campaign. A wine flagon, a dish, a box, or small vase of incense are seen on every occasion of sacrifice in the bas-reliefs. The smoke and crackling decided the success of the sacrifice. After this the priest ordered the *victimarius* to slaughter the animal. It was stunned and the head held upwards [69] if the sacrifice was to a god of the heavens, and the knife struck upwards from below; or the head was held downwards, and the animal was struck from above if the sacrifice was to a god of the inferno.

The blood was poured on the altar, the beast was incensed and sprinkled with wine and disjointed. The entrails could not be touched. They were taken out with knives and, if favourable, burnt. This action began with a libation of wine on the part of the officials, and the priest sprinkled the entrails with wine, meal and incense before consumption in the fire. The other portions of the animals belonged to the assisting priest. A cake made of *far* was always added to the burnt offerings, and various fruits representing the produce of first fruits of the earth. These are to be distinguished on many of the altars in these bas-reliefs. A sacrifice to propitiate Neptune was offered on the shore, as in No. LXIII., and the assistants stood with their feet in the water a certain way from the mark of the height of the tide. After this a circuit was made of the fleet in a boat so as to purify the entire expedition, and all engaged in it.

It will be noticed that the priests and assistants, one of whom is always a *camillus,* or youthful acolyte of noble

---

[69] See a bas-relief in the British Museum representing the sacrifice of a bull with the head in this position after being brought to its knees by a blow.

family in close personal attendance on the pontifex, are crowned with leaves. The dresses of the assistants have a fringe of gold, even those of the *popœ* and *victimarii*, these latter strip to the waist before immolating the victim, so as to save their dress from the risks of staining or pollution with blood.

The sacrifices generally take place in the front of the camp, in the Prætorian quarter. Besides the double flutes usually played, we see on more than one occasion both the *buccina* and the *tuba* sounding vigorously, so as to drown any sounds or interrupting voices, where the bystanders are composed of mixed multitudes, not only of troops of various nationalities, but of settlers, citizens, women, often including many Dacian and mixed races, inhabiting the military stations and colonies.

As the Roman held with all his might to the *exactness* of observances, to the accurate performance of every gesture, or even look, enjoined in the ancient books, the least particle of the rite was of the greatest importance, and had to be looked to with a painful accuracy and anxious vigilance. So that the gods must be *compelled to lend themselves to the will of man*, for instance, to desert a favoured city and give it as a prize to the besiegers. A single omission or word out of place attracted a guilt that required a special expiation, or made the repetition of the whole sacrificial act inevitable. It sometimes happened that a sacrifice had to be repeated 30 times, because a mistake had been made every time, or an unlucky circumstance had occurred.[70] But the inward intention, or the devotion of the heart, or even the indifference or incredulity of the worshipper, were matters not essential. According to Pliny[71] one priest was required to read or repeat the formula to the principal official, and a crowd of several will be noticed, ready to remind or prompt the emperor on every occasion on which the subject occurs on the column. They are all eagerly watching the actions of the sacrificing pontiff, and careful to remind him of every point as the ceremony goes on. Another priest had to keep silence amongst the hearers, and this is seen in the acts and gestures specially of one in the composition numbered No. LXV. Flutes were kept playing during the entire ceremony to prevent any other sound or word being heard. Experience had proved, according to Pliny, that as often as a noise or word of bad omen was heard during the repetition

---

[70] Döllinger, ib.   [71] II. N. 28.

of the prayers and the fulfilment of the required acts, or any error committed in the prayer itself, some calamitous augury was sure to be discerned in the entrails of the victim. Sometimes if after all ceremonies fulfilled, as at the death of Germanicus, sacrifice proved ineffectual, temples were pelted with stones, altars overthrown, or the *Lares* turned out of the house. In prayers of general importance affecting the welfare of the state, such as those offered during the war, Jupiter Capitolinus was first invoked. But it does not seem to have been always clear to which god the sacrifice should be offered, and in that case the form was "Be thou god or goddess!" Gods such as Jupiter, and goddesses as in a figure sculptured on the column thought to be Diana, Hecate, or Aurora, are invoked, whose help might be required by the rising of the moon or breaking of the day.

It was necessary to repeat the forms of words in some instances three times, in others nine. Vows were often pronounced in critical moments by the Romans, before a battle or storm out loud, so as to secure the favour of the deity and increase the fervour and confidence of troops.[72] Altars, temples, and the institution of public games were often vowed on such occasions. Many of the buildings and institutions of Trajan were probably fulfilments of vows made openly on such occasions. Sometimes great sacrifices, share in spoils, the best of the armour taken, festal games, libations, *lectisternia,* feasts of meat, &c., to the gods were then vowed. Trajan on his return and after his last Dacian war carried into execution such vows in the fullest manner. Ten thousand gladiators were paired in the amphitheatre, eleven thousand beasts were slain in sacrifices, and the public games and ceremonies lasted 120 days.[73] The sacrifices of the early Roman state had mostly been offered with reference to agriculture, and burnt corn, *confarreatio,* was one of the commonest offerings, though the beasts of the flock were the principal. These were sacrifices of atonement, and are the objects offered in the representations on the column. Besides sacrificing the life of the animal to satisfy the justice or vengeance of the gods, and offering corn, fruit, bread and wine, there was a furthur object in the death of animals, viz., the inspection of their entrails, from which auguries were obtained and inquiries made into the will of the gods.

---

[72] Non est meum si mugiat Africis malus procellis, ad miseras preces decurrere et votis pacisci, &c.—Hor. Od. iii. 29, 59.

[73] Dion. Cass. lxvii. 15.

AUGURIES.

The Emperor Trajan is usually seen holding a crooked staff in his hand, this is the *lituus*, (derived from *lito*, to obtain good auguries in the sacrifice), a divining rod.   The emperor had supreme authority, in his character of *Pontifex Maximus*, to interpret the auguries.   With this instrument the old *aruspices*, who divined from the flight of birds, used to mark off an imaginary division of the heavens, which had to be watched perhaps for twenty-four hours.   The Etruscans, however, were the most renowned *aruspices*, and introduced the *entispicia*, a most favourite and mystic system, by which all sorts of accidental convolutions of the entrails of victims were consulted.   The liver was an important organ : if the right lobe was wanting, if it shrunk in boiling, if some of the veins were very large, these were bad signs.   Fissures or indentations in the examined parts were of various interpretations.   Credence is said to have been given to superstitions of this astonishing kind, even since the renaissance in the sixteenth century. The old Romans pushed their superstitions on auguries to an incredible extent.   Not only entrails of victims, but prodigies, were eagerly consulted, and all were taken into careful consideration by the senate, and by rulers as exact and orthodox as Trajan.   Besides eclipses and other phenomena of the sun and moon, unusual rainbows, shooting stars, abortive births of man or beast were significant of good or evil.   " There were showers of stones, earth, chalk, and ashes, idols shed tears or sweated blood, oxen spoke, men were changed into women, cocks into hens,"[74] and other prodigies too numerous to mention, and all Rome waited for the interpretation of these wonders.   It will be readily understood that on a long and difficult expedition, accidents, surprises, unusual phenomena in the sky, or the earth, or in the water, were sure to occur, and that to satisfy his own mind and the superstitious fears of his troops, a wise commander, s.ich as Trajan, carefully made good his ground by the use of the resources at the command of the state religion.

---

[74] Döllinger, vii.

STATIONS FROM WHICH THE TROOPS WERE COLLECTED.

The forces which the Emperor Trajan collected for his first Dacian war, had been stationed, as I have said, partly amongst the legions and auxiliaries of his German army, partly on the Dacian frontier, and at the various fortified stations forming the military posts on the great roads from Germany through Pannonia, and along the Save, the southernmost tributary of the Danube, after the change in its direction from south to eastwards. Other forces came from Rome, such as the Prætorians. Most of the troops came from the north and north-west, and marched by the roads leading to and along the bank of the Save. That river is navigable as far as the confluence of the river Kulpa (the ancient Colapis), a distance of about 250 miles above its junction with the Danube. In the angle formed by the Kulpa and the Save was the fortress of Sistia, Segesta or Segestica (the modern Sisek), the great military arsenal of Pannonia Superior The place was protected by the two rivers, and further by a canal dug along the ground intervening between the two rivers. It is possibly represented more than once in the sculpture, particularly in the compositions in which Trajan is shown collecting troops and stores for the war from various riverside dockyards and arsenals. Apollodorus had seen this fortress often in his journeys between Rome and the borders of the Danube, over which he was employed to construct one, if not two, noble bridges.

Communication was easy between Segestica and the Adriatic shores. Good roads ran round the head of the gulf and between Ariminium (Rimini), Aquileia, and other military stations. Communication, too, was obtained still more easily for troops and material from Rome and the cities of Italy by Ancona, which Trajan formed into a military port, and where he subsequently built a triumphal arch. From Segestica the emperor was able to float down his various stores, arms and munitions of war, and horses and men were taken down to the Danube by the same route without doubt, during the first as well as during the second war (see the horse transports in No. XXIV.). Segestica was also the station of the river squadron of light armed Liburnian galleys and biremes, vessels with two banks of oars, which were kept in permanent commission by the emperor, in order to keep the river clear of hostile boats, and available at all times as a highway along the northern frontier. To this day Segesta, the modern town, contains ruins of much interest, and is still the port at which cargoes of corn grown in southern Hungary are discharged from the barges which bring them up the Save, vessels of from 100 to 250 tons burden.   These cargoes are conveyed up the Kulpa in boats, some of them of three tons burden as far as Karlstadt, and the same trade was probably active under the Roman rule.

It will be seen on reference to the lowest sculpture of the spiral, that the banks of the Save or Danube were carefully guarded and watched night and day, and that the stores accumulated on the shore banks were brought entirely by the river.   These stores are being discharged from boats. The banks of the river Save are still covered with forest. In the modern navigation one of the chief difficulties lies in the number of fallen trees or snags which pierce or beat in the bottoms of ill-built vessels descending the stream.   It is now navigated by steamers.

On account of these risks Trajan probably brought but few of his troops down this river, with the exception of detachments sent to protect the artillery and stores on their passage down the stream.   The Save is nearly two miles wide at the point of junction with the Danube, and there all these stores and troops awaited the arrival of the emperor.   He seems to have followed the roads leading from Germany, which take a course to some degree parallel to that of the Save, and touch on the stream of the Drave (Dravus) some distance above its junction with the Danube.   It was along this route that his German legionaries, *socii*, and auxiliaries, drawn from the large force permanently established in Germany, would march : troops with which he was personally acquainted, both officers and men—men who were thoroughly attached to his person.

It is doubtful what numbers were collected for the invading army.   Seven legions, comprising about six thousand men each, ten thousand Prætorians, a body of Batavian cavalry, and a mixed force of auxiliaries, some of whom were Germans, and are seen leading the attack in many battles as light troops and skirmishers, made up from sixty to perhaps eighty thousand men.[75]   It is probable that all these troops marched from the north, and had crossed the Save in small detachments by means of the large flotilla of vessels of transport, as well as of Liburnian galleys, which guarded the mouth of the river.

---

[75] Merivale, lxiii.

LINE OF MARCH.

Trajan passed all his troops in review at Singidunum, the modern Belgrade, which is on the angle formed by the two rivers and on the south side of the Save. From this point the united march of the invading army began. He led them first to the passage of the Morava, and so down the south bank of the Danube as far as Viminacium. There is no evidence of any bridge of boats in the sculpture earlier in the campaign than that over the Danube; but there are many rivers crossed with bridges of one kind or another in the course of these representations, and communications were probably made by some permanent wooden bridges over such streams as crossed the great military road. This road had been prepared as far as Viminacium in the time of Domitian, which place was fortified and was the head-quarters of the seventh legion at the time of the opening of the war.

At Viminacium (Kastolatz) the river expands into a broad stream, with a small island in the centre, and at this place the emperor determined to form a bridge of boats across the stream. This bridge is represented with accuracy in the sculpture, and a full description of it is given in the detailed account of the spiral of the shaft. The bridge was in two portions, as will be seen in the bas-relief, and the ends, at least on the Wallachian shore, were carefully carried to the bank on a permanent pier of timber supported on piles driven into the bed of the river. This was according to principles well understood by the Roman engineers, and accord with the instructions contained in Vegetius.

Opposite Kastolatz is Ujpalanka (new palisade), an Austrian fortified post still communicating with a stockaded redoubt on the island. It is worth observing that small stockaded guard houses, such as are seen at the beginning of the bas-reliefs, providing for the security of the Roman bank of the river, and for the safe custody of stores, night embarkations, &c., are very nearly reproduced or continued in the watch posts of the military frontier of Austria. They are huts of stone or wood. " All along the Hungarian banks," says Mr. Paget,[76] " at certain distances, perhaps half a mile apart, are small buildings sometimes made of wood, and reared on posts, or in other situations mere mud huts, before each of which stood a sentry on duty. They were the stations of the Hungarian frontier guard."

---

[76] Hungary and Transylvania, ii. 93.

MOUNTAIN PASSES.

At Viminacium the highlands begin on both banks of the
Danube. On the Dacian or Hungarian side, the southern
spurs of the Carpathians abut upon the river's edge, and a
corresponding barrier is formed on the Roman side by the
northern spurs of the Balkan. For thirty miles the waters,
which are more than a mile wide at Belgrade, are confined
to a narrow and rocky channel, and the rocks and rapids,
which, both in Trajan's time and in our own, make the
navigation dangerous, precluded the possibility of freely
using the river as the line of communication between the
points at which he meant the river to be crossed. Some
miles further on the river expands again, and somewhere
near the confluence of a small stream on the Hungarian
bank called the Tierna, Trajan caused another bridge of
boats to be made, and his army crossed the river at these
two places in two main divisions.

So long as the river is clear of the formidable barriers
produced by the mountains named, there are facilities for
roads along the banks. At Alt Moldava an excellent road
now runs along the banks of the river. Moldava lies at the
foot of the Carpathians, which thereabouts appear to close
the passage completely, and it is only on a near approach
that they are found to be cleft through by a channel worn
between two rocky walls. The river here loses three-fourths
of its width, and the waters become deep, and their velocity
formidable in proportion. At various points along the
heights, thus abutting like precipices on the river, are still
to be seen the remains of forts or towers built by Trajan to
protect the road he made. Some of these have been incor-
porated into, or have formed the foundations of mediæval
towers. The feudal castle of Golumbacz, still a noble
object, and planted on the summit of an all but inaccessible
crag, is believed by travellers to be built at least on Roman
foundations. At Drenkova, according to Paget, half a mile
below Golumbacz, are the remains of a square Roman fort
called Gradisca, built by Claudius, "and a chain of similar
fortifications all the way from this to Trajan's bridge."

It was along the face of this cliff on the Servian or
Roman side that Trajan carried a road for that portion of
the army he intended to pass the river at a part lower than
Viminacium, in his second Dacian war, if not in the first, at
which the bridge shown in the sculptures of the column
was constructed. Many parts of these rocks still show

signs of this wonderful road. Just below Kozlamare, Page found the following inscriptions above some of these signs in the rock, giving the names of two of the legions employed:

TR · CÆSARE · AUS·
AUGUSTO · IMPERATO
PONT · MAX · TR · POT · XXXV.
LEG · IIII · SYTH · ET · V · MACEDO.[77]

From this point numerous traces of the road are to be seen extending to a distance of some fifty miles along the face of these cliffs, and the nature of the place, as well as the structure required to meet the difficulties presented by such a passage, are explained by the accompanying woodcut from the column.

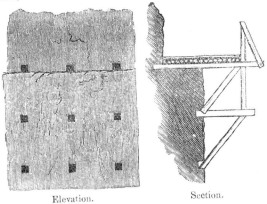

Elevation. Section.

Fig. 27.

Portions of the cliff were cut so as to form a narrow ledge or gallery wherever the face of the rocks rendered it impossible to dig such a pathway with pick and spade. "For the most part," says Mr. Paget, "the traces of the road now remaining," of which evidences are frequently visible on different parts of the rocks between Golumbacz and Orsova, "are reduced to a narrow ledge from two to six feet in width, cut in the solid rock at the height of ten feet above the high-water mark." This narrow ledge might, perhaps, in the time of Trajan, have sufficed for a towing path for mules or horses, such as are still employed on the course, and at the junction of the Theiss and the Temes, to drag barges laden with corn to Pesth and Vienna. Mr. Paget saw as many as forty-six horses and twenty men dragging a single barge up the stream.

The ledges, however, were enlarged by wooden galleries.
Below the ledge at regular distances, and in four distinct
elevations, as seen in the accompanying drawing, are holes
of about nine inches square, and eighteen deep.   Where the
rock hangs perpendicularly over the river, the ledge and the
holes may be traced very distinctly to a considerable distance
without intermission.   At other places they are interrupted
by a sloping bank, where an artificial road was no longer
required; and at others, where a slight chasm in the rocks
made it impossible to continue the ledge, a bridge seems to
have been thrown across.[78]   I give at page 69 a sketch of
the holes, and of the probable structure of the galleries as
furnished to Mr. Paget by M. Vásárhely, an engineer who
had explored and measured the holes.   Some portions of the
road were perhaps covered over with galleries.   This structure explains what seems incomprehensible in the inces-
sant short bridges required, sometimes, no doubt, over short
torrents, but frequently over gullies, and in the face of a
rock of which all the breaks and natural shelves seem to have
been grown over with oak timber.   In No. XLI. the reader
will see such a series of different wooden constructions, one
of which is an actual piece of roadway, under which logs are
laid crosswise with long timbers laid the reverse way over
them.   On this the workmen of the legionaries are laying
down a road of concrete.

Fig. 28.

---

[78] Paget, i. 122–3.

Trajan must have had this road prepared by the legions already quartered on the river side stations, for we can hardly suppose that works so difficult and extensive could have been executed actually during his march ; and the artist, in showing what the legionaries could do and had done, brings these operations into the current of his sculptured narrative, as he does the building of whole towns, with baths, theatres, &c. Some of which obviously could, at most, only have been founded and marked out during the war.

So effective and well chosen was the line and elevation of the road, with its immediate communication with the river, that it seems a question whether the modern Hungarians could do better than re-establish and enlarge it. " The rock having been cut away wherever it was called for, scarcely more than the restoration of the woodwork could have been necessary. Servia " (it is on the Servian bank) " would easily have supplied the timber ; the river would have transported it ; every Servian wears a hatchet."[79]

A coin commemorates the completion of the ' Via Trajana.' Near the end of the defile below which the river again opens out into a broad quiet stream opposite Old Gradisca, Mr. Paget saw the following inscription on a tablet sculpture on the wall of rock, and called ' Trajan's Tafel :'

IMP · CÆS · DIVI · NERVÆ · F.
NERVA · TRAIANVS · AUG · GERM.
PONTIF · MAXIMVS · TRIB · PO · XXX.

The tablet itself is oblong, and is supported by a winged genius on each side, " protected by the overhanging rock, which has been carved into a rich cornice surmounted by a Roman eagle ; on either side is a dolphin."[80] It has been much defaced both by time and by fires burnt beneath it by the Servian boatmen and fishermen. Here the rapids come to an end, the river becomes wide, and its waters still, and here the *second bridge* of boats was constructed. Here also end the precipitous sides of the river. The hills, or rocky strata, which form the barriers called the Iron-gate at a lower point, do not abut on the river with lofty sides, such as are seen in the channel of the rapids.[81]

---

[79] Quarterly Rev. in Handbook for S. Germany.
[80] Travels, ii. 121.
[81] " The name *Iron-gate* would lead one to expect a narrow pass closed in by mountains, but the reality does not correspond with the name, for the banks of the river, so far from being contracted and precipitous, are here formed by round-backed slate hills, sloping gradually upwards away from the water's edge. It is merely the translation of the words by which the Turks, in their

Mr. Paget states that he was informed of the cutting of a canal at this critical spot by the Romans, and that remains of it are still to be traced, but he had no opportunity of verifying this report in person.[82] The hills below the rapids retire in a northerly direction from the banks of the river in two ranges, and in the narrow valley between runs the river Tierna (Tjerna). Here the second in command, perhaps Lucius Quietus, the Moor, formed a bridge of boats which was kept as a permanent ferry over the river, and the second column of the imperial army here crossed into Dacia.

The valley through which this small river runs is separated by a chain of hills on the left or western side from the alluvial plains, watered by the Tibiscus or Temes, and still further west by the larger stream of the Theiss. The military road by which this portion of the army marched leads for some way to the right of these hills, then ascends them and descends upon and joins the road that runs along the Tibiscus, or Temes, (leading to Tibiscus, the modern Temesvar,) at a station near Karansebes at the point of junction of the Temes and Bistra.

The army led by Trajan himself has been sometimes supposed to have followed a more westerly course, and to have ascended the valley of the Theiss. But this is doubtful for, if so, it will be seen that he must have turned back or struck eastwards, avoiding the marshy land that lies between the Tibiscus and the Tisia (Theiss). He, perhaps, took measures to keep the river Theiss as a defence on his flank. This river is navigable as far as Tokay. Trajan had, perhaps, a force to guard this river, which only ascended to Singidava, the modern Szeged or Segedin, the point at which it receives the water of the Mariscus, Maros, along the fertile valleys of which river lay the pastures that enriched the Dacian sheep owners.[83] No permanent road, however, seems to have been

---

fondness for metaphor, designate a spot difficult to cross, which shuts in, as it were, the navigation of the river. The rocks on each side and in the bed of the river forming the *Iron-gate* are a hard micacious slate, very difficult to break or blast, which would present very serious obstacles to the project of cutting a canal along the Servian shore. At the beginning of summer these rocks are nearly covered, and large steamers usually pass down them at that season, favoured by the height of the water."—Handbook of Southern Germany, p. 542.

[82] Travels, ii. 125.

[83] Long barge-like vessels come down the Theiss from Szegedin. These are clean, well-built boats, " covered in with a kind of deck" (much like the boats in the lower part of the column), " and chiefly employed in bringing up " corn from the country of the Theiss and the Temes to Pesth and Vienna."— Paget, ii. 81.

established along the Theiss as the banks are long and marshy, and are liable to frequent if not yearly inundations, and the popular tradition that Trajan followed the course of that river must be received with caution. On the other hand, a regular road was made and maintained along the course of the Tibiscus as well as the shorter road separated from it by hills, which has been already mentioned. And it is probably along the plain, watered by the Temes or Tibiscus, rather than the banks of the Theiss that Trajan must have marched. A few words only remain of a commentary written on the war by Trajan himself, but these words make it clear from the stations named that this was the road he followed. The words are,—" Inde Berzobim, deinde Aixi, processimus. Bersovia, xii. ; Ahitis, iii. ; Caput Bubali, x. ; Tivisco." [84] A third road was made in the course of the second Dacian war, and I will give the stations of these three roads together further on in these pages.

The gorge of the Bistra, which the united army entered, leads direct to the pass properly called that of the iron gate, which opens on the valley of the Maros close to the capital city of Decebalus. This narrow gorge is said to have been actually closed by gates of iron at the time of Trajan's expedition.

---

[84] Francke, Gesch. Trajans, 106.

THE FIRST WAR.

The Roman armies then united made themselves masters of the city of Zermizegethusa[85] after fighting their way against frequent and occasionally desperate resistance along the roads above mentioned. Decebalus retired before them with a large army in the direction of the Mariscus. The Dacians seem to have fought in the manner of barbarous nations of all ages, mainly by ambuscades and surprises, and by defending the forests and passes through which the Roman armies had to move. They were at the same time far from ignorant of some of the principles of those arts of war, least easily mastered by half civilised tribes, namely the manufacture and use of artillery, and systems of fortifications very formidable and difficult to capture, such as are described in detail in a former section. They are represented in the bas-reliefs as showing great cruelty to their prisoners, whose heads are seen stuck on lances along their lines of fortification, and whose bodies are seen bound to posts and cartwheels, as in No. XXXIII., and tormented by the women, who apply firebrands to their bare flesh. On the other hand, the Roman soldiers cut off the heads of their opponents, bringing them in triumph to show their beloved emperor, so as to claim the reward of personal prowess ; and in No. XVI., the earliest general action, a Roman legionary is seen holding a human head by the hair in his teeth while he continues fighting furiously. Generally Trajan strictly forbade plundering and insult on the part of his own soldiers, a fact known to Decebalus, who justly considered it as making the moral effect of the Roman advance only the more formidable.[86]

In the course of the march the Burri, a people settled on the banks of the Theiss, sent a message to Trajan, written in Latin, on a large *fungus*, which has been thought by some to be commemorated in the bas-relief, No. V., in which they advise the emperor to forego his design, but to which no answer was returned.

The emperor advanced, as will be seen in the bas-reliefs, making good his road, establishing entrenched camps as future fortified stations, and securing himself on one height after another. Many of these were already strong places in possession of the Dacians, and were attacked and carried

---

[85] "Zarmi-tzeket-kusa-mansion couvert de peaux."—Bergmann, Les Gètes, in Merivale.

[86] Dion Cass. lxviii. 7.

sword in hand. Lucius Quietus gained great advantages on the parallel line of march.[87] Meanwhile Decebalus sent messengers and envoys, first of inferior, then of superior feudal or military rank,[88] to attempt some kind of delay or diversion. Sura and Claudius Livianus were sent by the emperor to confer with Decebalus, whose object was to satisfy the Roman army without being reduced to the destruction of his strongholds or the surrender of his capital. But nothing came of these negociations. The ambassadors of the Dacian kings are known in the sculptures by their sheepskin cap, the token of their nobility.

Trajan at last brought the forces of Decebalus to bay at a place of which it is not easy to point out the site. It was beyond the Tibiscus and near Tapæ, the field on which Julianus had repulsed the Dacians in the reign of Domitian. Here Decebalus was defeated with great slaughter. Trajan suffered considerable losses, and as surgeons and bandages were wanting, he is said to have torn his *paludamentum* to strips, in order to supply this want to his wounded soldiers.[89] This incident is commemorated on the bas-relief composition, No. XXVIII. Popular tradition still points to a place called Crossfeld, near Thorda, as the field of battle, which is called *Prat Trajan* (Trajan's field) to this day. Merivale considers this as too far in the interior of Dacia for the real field of battle, and warns his readers against trusting too much to the modern name.

The Dacians took refuge in various fortified ports, as will be seen in the bas-reliefs. To these they were followed by the Romans, whom Trajan pushed vigorously in advance, to make the utmost use of their advantage. All the strongholds were taken by escalade, or with the use of the *testudo*. Most of them seem to have been built, in a great measure, of wood, protected by hides, and to have been fired by the Roman solders. Maximus, another of Trajan's generals, succeeded in capturing a fortified *oppidum* of the Dacians, and seized the sister of Decebalus. Finally Trajan became master of the last of the fortified places of Decebalus, of which the name has not been preserved. Here he found the treasure, the arms, and the engines of war made by the help, or after the teaching of Roman engineers. More valuable still was the eagle taken from the Roman

---

[87] Dion Cass.]xvii. 8.

[88] Πιλοφόρων, Dion Cass.

[89] οὐδὲ τῆς 'εαυτοῦ εσθῆτος λέγεται φείσασθαι 'αλλ' ἐς τα λαμπάδια ἀυτην κατατεμεῖν. Dion Cass. lxviii. 8.

general Fuscus, and of which the staff is seen carried from the beginning of the war in the bas-reliefs.[90] In this stronghold were found also workmen and engineers of war-like machines (μηχανοποιούς), captured or seduced from the Romans ; and one of the conditions imposed by the emperor was the delivery of these persons, as well as of Roman deserters, of whom there were probably many, who had been induced to come over to the Dacians as instructors in building and other mechanical arts. Decebalus was required to raze the walls of his strongholds, to retire from portions of country seized during his own reign, to hold the enemies of the empire as his own, and to agree not to allow any more desertions from the Roman frontiers. Zermizegethusa was deserted,[91] and Ulpia Trajana, a colony named after the emperor, was founded on or close to the site of it. These conditions are represented in the final composition relating to the first war in the bas-reliefs. Decebalus kneels as a suppliant, and the notables of his court and country throw down their shields and weapons in token of unconditional surrender to the clemency of the emperor. Some of these personages are seen with hands bound behind them, either prisoners not yet released by the Romans, or persons reserved to grace the imperial triumph in Rome. There the Dacian deputies or prisoners appeared with clasped hands before the senate,[92] Decebalus yielded formal possession to the conquerors of the places taken during the war, and peace was concluded.

Trajan entrusted the care of the conquered places and of the Roman peace to a garrison of legionaries whom he established at Ulpia Trajana, and before his departure for Rome he is seen on the column giving his final instructions to the officers, no longer in armour, but dressed in the toga of Roman citizens in time of peace.

The sculptures on the column wind up the subjects descriptive of this war with a stately composition representing Victory between two trophies of arms. It is fully described in its place, and it is worth notice that this grace-ful figure exactly represents the attitude and the action of the arms and hands of the statue of the Louvre in Paris, known as the Venus de Milo.

---

[90] ὅπλα, μηχανήματα, ᾿αιχμάλωτα, τό τε σημεῖον. Dion Cass. lxviii.
[91] Dion Cass. lxviii.
[92] Dion Cass. lxviii.

The interval between the two Dacian Wars.

Trajan returned to Rome, and was honoured by the senate with the title of *Dacicus.* Dion Cassius and Pliny bear witness to the enthusiasm of the Romans at the return of a monarch whose entire conduct had endeared him so much to all classes of the citizens. He declined the honours of a triumph, and entered the city on foot, distinguished by his stature, being a head taller than the generality of his soldiers, and bare-headed, as he is usually represented on the column. Every portico, cornice, wall, and ledge on which a footing could be had in the streets through which the procession passed were crowded with eager spectators.

To reward the army and increase the general joy, Trajan held one of the greatest exhibitions seen for a long period of gladiatorial combats, public games, and sacrifices. Dancers were again introduced into the theatres, and Trajan seems to have taken a personal pleasure in restoring an entertainment which other Roman rulers had the grace to have banished from the public shows.

When these festivities were ended, Trajan devoted himself to the most diligent supervision, and to a large share in the personal administration of public affairs. For civil administration he had both talent and sagacity. Though given to gross debauchery, he had the wisdom to give general orders that no commands given after prolonged drinking bouts should be executed, at any rate, immediately.[93] He rose after these excesses and devoted himself to the hearing of causes and the diligent administration of justice, entered into the details of the civil administration, and originated many wise and prudent measures specially for the bringing up of orphans and the poor, the improvement of land and police, and the rebuilding and adornment of the cities and harbours of the Empire.[94]

---

[93] Victor. Cæs. 13.   [94] Merivale.

PREPARATION FOR A SECOND WAR.

During these peaceful labours the restless ambition of
Decebalus again threatened the Roman occupation. The
first sign of disturbance seems, according to Dion,[95] to have
been an expedition against the Jazyges across the Theiss.
Roman and other deserters were again seduced to his pay,
and probably engineers amongst the number. Trajan determined on reducing this turbulent province. The Senate
declared these rebels public enemies, and exhorted the em
peror to use all the power of the state in bringing them into
subjection. Trajan at once determined to undertake a second
war in person, and this time to do the work of subjection
and annexation thoroughly.

---

[95] Dion Cass. lxviii. 10.

Fig. 29.

Meanwhile, one great bridge over the Danube below the iron gates, had been constructed by Apollodorus at the point at which a bridge of boats had been in use from the opening of the first campaign.

Remains of this bridge still exist, though we cannot accept the measurements of Dion Cassius,[96] or his statement that twenty piers on which the bridge was built were made of squared stone, each pier 150 feet in height, exclusive of the foundation; 60 feet broad; and the arches of 170 feet span, and built of hewn masonry. The bridge was built by Apollodorus, the architect of the forum and column, and an accomplished engineer. It was made however of timber, with the single exception of two arches on the southern, and probably two corresponding on the northern extremity, the two stone arches are uneven in height and width, and both are of much smaller span than the wooden arches.

The measurement of Dion Cassius would be—

$$
\begin{array}{ll}
\text{20 arches, 170 feet} & \text{-} \quad \text{-} \quad \text{-} \quad \text{3,400} \\
\text{And, say, 19 piers, of 60 feet each} & \text{-} \quad \text{1,140}
\end{array}
$$

or 4,540 feet. In this calculation the abutments on the two banks are not included. As seen, sculptured in the column, from which the accompanying woodcut is taken, it is evident that the bridge was made of timber with arched girders, each series having triple beams of solid timber, of large scantling and held together by cross pieces of equal solidity, material easily cut in the forests that then clothed the banks both of the Save and the Danube. Only two arches on each end were of stone and arched, and they are represented as less in span than the wooden arches. It is curious that Dion Cassius, who held a provincial government at no great distance, should have made the statement he did, but the bridge had been destroyed, and it is probable that he gave his measurements only from hearsay, and that the 60 feet assigned to the widths of the piers were measurements actually taken from those which formed the abutment on the two banks, and were accessible in his time. Count

[96] Dion Cass. lxviii. 13.

Marsigli estimates the entire length to be 2,758 feet, and
considers that the width of the piers must have been
exaggerated.   The piers only were of stone or concrete.[97]
  If, then, the width of the 20 piers are taken off from the
total actual length, it will be evident that whatever be the
measurement of the wooden arches, they could not have
much exceeded 100 feet in span, and their construction
would be by no means an impossibility.   The arches consist of three concentric curved beams composed of four
lengths each, tied together by four transverse timbers.
Each length was perhaps built up of many pieces in the
method usual with Roman engineers (and still in use in
Rome for constructing the uprights of heavy scaffolding,
p. 42), both on the arches and on the timber abutments
constructed for them.   The probable construction of the
roadway was the same as we show in the accompanying
woodcut of the bridge thrown by Cæsar over the Rhine.[98]

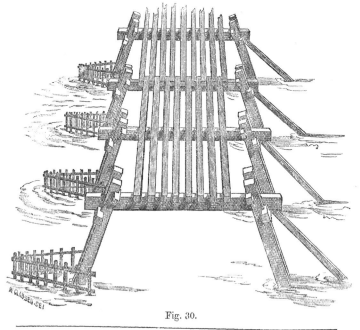

Fig. 30.

[97] " Tout le reste n'est qu'une grande et belle charpente."—Crevier, His-
toire des Empereurs, Francke, p. 132.   Mr. Paget estimates the width of the
river from end to end of the remains of the bridge to be 3,900 feet, or 1,300
yards, but this seems to be only the rough estimate given by guides and guide-
books, and he had no means of verifying this computation.
  [98] The woodcut in the text is from the Architecture of Palladio, Book iii. v.
It can also be seen in a more picturesque form in the recent representation of
the Jules César of the Emperor Napoleon III.

Mr. Paget describes the remains of the bridge as they now are. There are two massive embankments at the beginning of the causeway, and 13 out of the 20 piers can still be seen when the water is low in summer. They are of concrete made up with large stones, and may have been cased with hewn masonry. The spot chosen is about five miles below Skala Gladova, the first place below the rapids at which the Danube is free from a rocky bed. According to Dion., the bed of the river is of mud at this point, but modern travellers agree in stating that it is of gravel. According to Count Marsigli, the depth of the river in summer is not great at this point, nowhere more than 18 feet, and he considers the building of such a bridge by no means a triumph of engineering audacity, *far less difficult* a feat than the Pont du St. Esprit built by the freemasons over the Rhone. A bridge of wood of 250 feet span crosses the Portsmouth river in North America.—(Sir H. Douglas, in Tredgold's Bridges, 233.) There has, however, been no bridge built since so low down the Danube. On the opposite or southern shore stood Severinum, the modern Sozoreny, a strong rampart or wall of brick and gravel, measuring 420 feet by 162 feet, near which on a conical mound is a mutilated tower.[99] The southern end was also flanked by a fort, and this is seen in the sculpture on the column.

This bridge was on one of the high roads from the southern provinces into Dacia. The road was continued down the side of the river till it reached a point opposite to the junction of the Aluta with the Danube. Here, at a place called Gieli, are still ruins of two forts similar in position and purpose to the two that protected the two ends of the bridge just described. Here also in the summer, when the water is low, the remains of a row of piers of masonry may still be made out, and are traceable indeed at other times by the eddies of the water. A road, of which the remains are still traceable, ran northwards from this point and parallel with the course of the river Aluta.[100]

[99] Handbook S. Germany, 543.

[100] The road from Viminacium, the westernmost and nearest point of contact of Trajan's line of march, and subsequent route into Dacia, ran by Arcidava, Centum Puteæ, Bersovia, Azizis, Caput Bubali, Tiviscum (the modern Temesvar).

The next road crossed the bridge of Trajan below the iron gates at Orsova and followed the valley of the Czerna to Mehadia, along the valley of the Temes, crossed the valley of the iron gate. It then crossed the plain of Hâtzeg by Hunyod, Varhely, mounted the hill of Deva, and descended on the valley of the Maros, a tributary of the Theiss. Thence it proceeded to Karlsburg, Thorda, and Maros Vasarheli. The Roman stations were, Tierna, Ad Mediam, Mehadia (the baths of Hercules), Ad Pannonios, Gaganæ, Masclianæ, Tiviscum, Agnavæ, Pons Augusti, Zermizegethusa, Adaquas, Germizera, Blandiana, Apula, Brucla, Salinæ, Patavissa, Napoca, Optatiana, Langiana Cersie, Parolissum.

From these three points, Viminacium, the Pons Trajani, and the line of the Aluta, Trajan had constructed and maintained well engineered and well protected roads, so as to be able at any time to pour troops into provinces so vast and important of which he knew the wealth both in soil and minerals ; as well as their value as a barrier against the northern barbarians and populations ; and from which he foresaw good troops and faithful subjects could be made for the Roman empire.

All his preparations had been carefully planned and systematically carried out from the very outset of the first war. Besides the route along the valley of the Iron gate, in which had been the stronghold to which Decebalus retreated after the capture of his capital in the first war, Trajan had two other routes opened out and now ready for his military operations. They led to two other passes further eastward, those of the Vulkan, and the Rothenthurm.

The third route followed the course of the Aluta as far as the pass of the Rothenthurm and Karlsburg, on which road was Apula, the capital of the mining district. The stations were, Drubetis, Amutria, Pelendova, Castra Nova, Romula, Acidava, Rusidava, Pons Aluti, Burridava, Castra Trajana, Arutela, Prætorium, Pons vetus Stenarum, Cedonie, Acidava, Apula.

SECOND DACIAN WAR.

The emperor prepared for war with the whole power at his command. This seems to have spread consternation among the chiefs of the tribes whom Decebalus had leagued together in his defence, and many of them made their submission to the emperor. The Dacian chieftain tried to obtain terms for himself but seems to have been unwilling to make a complete submission and lay down his arms. According to Dion.,[1] he sent spies or envoys into Mœsia to meet the emperor on his advance, and put an end to the war by assassinating him, he being accessible to all applicants ; but this plot was discovered by one of the men employed who was put to the torture and confessed. The two heads of these spies are supposed to be figured in one of the bas-reliefs relating to this war now on the arch of Constantine in Rome, but taken from the triumphal arch of the Forum of Trajan. Two Dacian heads are also seen on spears planted in the ground in No. XLI., evidently those of spies, for Trajan would not suffer prisoners or country people to be put to death, but the scene in which these two ghastly trophies figure belongs to the first Dacian war. Decebalus then entrapped Longinus, a Roman general whom he invited to a parley, and treacherously placed him in confinement, offering him freedom as the price of his disclosure of the plans of Trajan. Longinus refused and Decebalus then detained him as a hostage, offering to release him if the Romans would grant him terms, of which the possession of the whole country to the Danube, together with repayment of the costs of the war were leading conditions. Dion. Cassius seems to leave us in uncertainty as to Trajan's answer, but Longinus found means to send a freedman under pretext of a missive to the emperor favourable to the adoption of the proposed terms, but urging him to continue the war with vigour, and having done this he took poison and so relieved Trajan of anxiety on his account. Decebalus offered to exchange the body of Longinus for the person of the messenger, but the emperor refused to deliver the man to his vengeance in exchange for the dead general, and determined on the destruction of Decebalus and the complete subjugation of Dacia.

It is probable that Trajan collected all the troops he could gather or could spare from Italy and the various stations on either shore of the Adriatic, and that these

---

[1] lxviii. 11.

troops were transported in the second campaign as far as
they could be taken by sea. Not only does Trajan figure
in the sculptures of the second war as going from one
colony to another on the riverside stations (as no doubt he
did), but, in more than one, large ships are represented with
sails, anchors, and other evidence of sea-going equipments.
Some of the ports at which he embarks or disembarks have
piers and lighthouses.   In others, waves are represented
breaking against the sea wall of the place.   In No. XXIV.,
one would suppose his triumphal arch on the mole of the harbour of Ancona was represented, as perhaps it is.   He is
personally present during these operations in the sculptures.
He is welcomed on his landing; sacrifices are offered to
Neptune on his behalf, *e.g.*, in No. LXIII.   At the military
stations and colonies the entire population, soldiers and
civilians, men, women and children, turn out to welcome
a ruler who seems to have been so justly and so universally
loved.

The war was prosecuted with vigour.   Trajan is seen
sacrificing to inaugurate his new bridge.   Here the emperor
seems to have crossed at the head of the main body of
his army.   At the lower bridge another force crossed, and
perhaps a third had advanced in the direction of Zarmizegethusa, or Ulpia Trajana, over the bridge of boats formerly stationed to join the mouth of the Tierna with
the southern bank.   It is from the bridge itself strangely
enough that there is no road traceable on the map,
and it is possible that the transit over the river was made
there, and that a road was afterwards made up the northern
bank for the short distance between the bridge head and the
course of the Tierna.   The easternmost line of march lay, as
I have said already, along the line of the Aluta.   The
Romans ascended it to its source in the western Carpathians,
and crossing over the pass of the Rothenthurm descended
with irresistible impetus into the fertile plains watered by
the Mariscus.

Trajan seems to have driven Decebalus in this war to the
mountain fastnesses of Transylvania.   He is seen in the bas-
relief occupying and fortifying rocky heights and places
difficult to attack.   On the other hand the Romans watch
the Dacians from temporary or permanent forts, and Trajan
developed all his military knowledge and engineering skill
in mechanical artillery and the other resources of antique
siege operations.   It is remarkable that in this second war
most of the actions of importance are fought under the
walls of strong places.   The Dacians seem never to have

been bold enough to venture out of reach of such refuges in cases in which defeat was anticipated from the first. Sometimes the Romans follow them in and desperate hand to hand conflicts are seen carried on within the entrenchments; sometimes these places are carried by storm. Occasionally the Dacians try with desperate valour and the use of their shields as a *testudo* to carry Roman positions by storm, and as there were in places small garrisons which would have been in considerable danger, and some of them may have been overpowered. Often the Romans are protected only by wooden fortifications made of logs of timber.

At last the Romans reached the great stronghold of Decebalus, which seems to have been built on a height, partly on scarped rocks; to have had walls faced with masonry, held together by layers of timber passing through the thickness of the walls to hold them together and better resist the drag of the Roman *falx*, or drawhook, with which, when once a stone could be displaced by mining, the masonry round it could be torn out by the assailing force. Against this fortress attempts at storming are seen to be ineffectual, though great valour must have been shown by the Romans, as represented in the sculptures. A number of siege engines were also employed in vain, and are seen abandoned. At last a breach at one angle of the fort and a desperate action, either with the garrison who issue out or with a relieving force, opened a way to the Romans. The Dacian nobles in despair fired the houses of their other towns and drank poison. Decebalus seems to have made one or two more desperate efforts, and at last is seen to stab himself. His head was taken to the emperor's quarters, and most of the chiefs then made their final submission. The few scattered fortresses, and bands still under arms, were captured and dispersed by the Roman cavalry.[2]

The treasures of Decebalus (seen in mule loads of precious cups and vessels) were found in a cavern under the river: according to Dion., the Sargetia or *Strehl*, in which statement, however, there is a confusion between Zarmizegethusa, the first Dacian capital, and the place to which he finally retreated, which may have been much further north.

According to the same author captives or slaves had been employed to construct the cavern or vault in the bed of the river, having temporarily turned the stream aside, and were destroyed by Decebalus as soon as it was done, in order that

---

[2] See ante, page 17.

his secret might be kept secure.   But it was betrayed to Trajan.[3]

This long resistance exhausted and went far to depopulate the country.   Trajan planted Roman colonies in their place, and invited settlers from other parts of the empire.   Four principal colonies were founded.   Ulpia Trajana commemorated in coins and inscriptions, is now to be traced by arched roofs, vaulted chambers, and remains of a temple and theatre [4] at a place called Varhely.   Apulum,[5] Colonia Apulensis, on the site of which is Karlsburg, is in the upper valley of the Maros.   It was the mining capital and the seat of a *Collegium Aurariorum.*   Napuca, the most northern, is on the site of the modern Maros Vasarhely [6] and Cerna or Dierna, on the small river Tjerna, near Mehadia, the site of the mineral baths of Hercules. Other towns were founded on the river Danube and, thus defined, the new province stretched from the Danube and the Theiss on the south and west, to the Carpathians on the north.   How far east it is difficult to say, perhaps to the Pruth.   Francke, and others think possibly as far as the Don.

The Dacians thus mixed became loyal subjects and firm friends of the emperor.   Hadrian, in the following reign, broke down the bridge from jealousy, or more probably, in accordance with a less warlike, certainly a less far-sighted policy.   Nevertheless, the Dacians remained true in their towns and stations, even while hordes of northern barbarians were pouring past them into Rome.   What they became under Trajan they still seem to remain.

In 1782 Mr. Chishull describes the Wallachs as "ordinarily calling themselves *Romans,* and their province, Tzerra Romanesca, being persuaded that they are descended of that original.   And in favour of this opinion they may allege their language, which is a broken mixture of Latin and Italian, into which have been accidentally adopted some few Turkish and Sclavonic words.—Even the vulgar sort," he says in another place, " usually speak Latin."

" They write entirely the Cyrillian Sclavonic character, which seems to be a detortion from the Greek ; and these properties of their language, as well as the characters, they have in common with Moldavia, which two provinces,

[3] Dion. lxviii. 14.   [4] Paget, Hungary, &c.
[5] Many inscriptions from Ulpia Trajana are preserved. Several were seen by Mr. Chishull in the market place of Hermanstadt, identifying it with Ulpia Trajana.
[6] Francke, Gesch. Trajans, 173.

together with Transylvania, constituted the ancient Dacia.
The two former, *Ripensis,* and the last, *Mediterranea."* [7]

The Dacian character of features in the Wallachs seems
to have struck Chishull. Mr. Paget, too, says :—" It is
impossible not to be struck with the resemblance of the
Wallach peasants to the Dacians of the Trajan column.
The dress, the features, and the whole appearance of the
Wallachs were so Dacian that a man fresh from Rome could
scarcely fail to recognise it. They have the same arched
nose, deeply sunken eye, and long hair, the same sheepskin
cap, the same shirt bound round the waist and descending
to the knees, and the same long loose trousers, which the
Roman chain is so often seen encircling at the ankles. It
only required to change the German or Hungarian over-
looker in his smart hussar uniform for the soldier of the
Roman legion in his brilliant armour" (this is a considerable change), "and we might have supposed ourselves,"
&c.[8]

The women, according to Mr. Chishull, seem to have
draped themselves still more nearly in the manner of the
Dacians seen in the sculptures representing the second war.
" The inferior sort of women are usually dressed when
abroad in a long and loose black mantle, reaching from
their shoulders down to the ground, and all round gathered
into deep and numberless folds, not unlike the gowns worn
by the islanders in the archipelago."[9]

As for the country, the plains are among the richest
pasture land in Europe. The account we are about to quote
is confirmed by those of Paget and modern books of travels
and guide books. What our author says, however, of the
absorption of gold dust in the grapes and vine tendrils of
Tokay, might be better understood perhaps as a figure of
speech of the incomparable vines of that district on the
banks of the Theiss.

" Besides all kinds of grain which grow on the surface
of the earth in Transylvania, it abounds with veins of
metals, minerals, and fossils of all sorts, particularly gold.
Among other fossils the native cinnabar is most rare, and
the quicksilver which is here found to perfection. Salt is dug
in several places "—in square stones or blocks—" by which
a large revenue accrues to the emperor. The reports (as to
gold) related by some, who were eye-witnesses both here (in
Transylvania) and at Toquay are very remarkable, of which

---

[7] Chishull's Travels, Journey from Adrianople to Holland, &c., p. 85.
[8] Travels, ii. 125.
[9] Chishull's Travels, 106.

I only mention the following :—A piece of gold is said to have grown to a vine, instead of the green tendril, by which it takes hold of the adjoining trees, or other substance that supports it.   Pure gold was found in a grape, instead of its ordinary natural stone.   Small gold drops were observed to adhere to the skin of a grape, and even an entire grape had been seen to consist of a perfect coat of gold." [10]

Trajan is supposed to have had Hadrian, his successor, with him in the second war ; and it is said that in the bas-reliefs in which Trajan is represented after having crossed his new bridge, Hadrian is represented.   He was constantly with the emperor, though his adoption as son did not take place till immediately before Trajan's death, if, indeed, it ever took place at all.

---

[10] Chishull's Travels, 103.

TRAJAN RETURNS FROM THE SECOND DACIAN WAR.

The emperor returned to Rome this time to celebrate a triumph and games on a scale of unexampled splendour. Dion. assures us that the games lasted 120 days, as already stated, that 11,000 head of cattle were killed, and that 10,000 gladiators fought in the circus. He returned to his supreme government, and planned and carried out many wise measures. Here we will take leave of Trajan. His later deeds, his Parthian wars, his death at Selinus in the year 117, belong to history. He was wise in council, farsighted in policy, sagacious in dealing with men, unsuspicious, generous, and tolerant; an able strategist, brave, humane, patient, active, tolerant of hunger and thirst, with all the qualities that make up the Pagan hero. He was a sportsman, a boon companion, not above the grossest vices of his age, never cruel except to the Christians and Jews. "He was," says Merivale, "the last of the emperors who ruled the empire in the spirit of an old Roman, viz., for the benefit of the Roman and Italian people." His portrait is familiar to us from a number of statues (see p. 7). His head is square and compact, the forehead broad, and well covered with hair, the lower jaw long, the chin small, the nose large but well cut, the eyes set in, the lips fine, and compressed, with a general expression of firmness and decision. His remains were placed in a golden vase, either in the hand of his statue, or under the base of the column.[11]

While biographies and histories are scanty, and the Roman forum hidden under 40 feet of loam and debris, that of Trajan under 12 or 14, the only full and detailed history of his Dacian war stands erect and substantially unchanged.

---

[11] Burton, Antiquities of Rome, 167.

ROMAN ART UNDER TRAJAN.

The height and size of the column of Trajan exemplify, no doubt, incongruities and violations of the principle of architectural propriety, yet it is one among the noblest monuments as well as the most valuable historical records of antiquity. A column enlarged to the proportions of a tower, with stylobate cornices, base, torus, capital, and other architectonic members, with no weight to carry, is an anomaly. A structure so solid and so lofty intended as the pedestal of a statue, though that statue be 20 feet high, might be a notion borrowed from the Greeks,[12] but could have been imagined by no Greek artist of better times on such a scale as we here see it. Much of the sculpture and all the composition is stiff and graceless, though each individual figure is incomparably faithful to life, and has all the qualities that give so high a place to the sculptured portraiture of the Imperial time in Rome till long after the age of Trajan. It is worth notice that the small figures of periods in decay of art often retain an excellence and dignity that are wanting in sculptures on a large scale, such as the basreliefs now on the arch of Constantine. We may take the column and its sculptures as the last great achievement of the classic period. Such as it is, however, it contains the only record we possess of an important conquest of imperial Rome, and is the principal source of our knowledge of the military equipment, armament, and engineering skill of the Roman legions. For much light on this part of the subject we are indebted to the late emperor of the French, Napoleon the Third,[13] who has not only written on the subject after careful and costly research, but caused these engines to be reproduced in many forms and tested at the French artillery ranges, as stated above. Further he had picked men from his army trained to throw the *pilum,* and in other ways to prove what the effect of the weapons of the legionary really was. Nothing in historic sculpture is more vivid and exact than these representations of antique warfare, battles, sieges, and marches, or truer than the portraiture of the Roman and the Wallach : life-like according to the narratives of modern travellers even at the present day.

The minuteness of historic sculpture to be seen at so great an elevation is a serious defect. It is to be remem-

---

[12] Plin. Hist. Nat. XXXVI. 6.
[13] Le passé et l'avenir de l'Artillerie, Vie de Jules César.

bered, however, that the column could be seen from the upper story of the Basilica, perhaps from upper windows of the two libraries, forming two other sides of the space in which the column stood. Further I must remind the reader that the column was coloured and gilt, so that the figures stood out in strong relief, and that the climate of Italy and the transparent air of Rome make fine lines and forms easy to examine at the distance of 300 or 400 feet, which are misty and indistinguishable in London at 40. The work will be but very partially seen in the museum from the different galleries, and most students of antiquity will regret that it cannot be thoroughly seen and carefully studied.

A FEW WORDS AS TO THE LATER HISTORY OF THE
COLUMN.

Alexander Severus is said to have ornamented the forum
with statues of illustrious men.   The forum was still entire
in the time of Constantine, who made merciless use of the
old sculptures for his own triumphal arch.   Ammianus
Marcellinus, in his account of the entry of the Emperor
Constans into Rome, A.D. 356, says that when "he came
to the forum of Trajan, a structure which I conceive to be
unique in the world, and deserving the admiration even of
celestial beings; he was struck with astonishment, casting
his thoughts over its gigantic edifices, which it is impossible
to describe, or for any mortals to imitate.   Giving up,
therefore, all hopes of attempting anything similar, he said
that the only thing he could or would imitate was the horse
on which the Emperor sat.   Upon which Hormisdas of the
royal family of Persia, who was near him, said, 'First order
a stable to be built similar to this, if you have the means:
may the horse to which you purpose forming have as extensive success as that which we are looking at!'"   The
forum escaped the ravages of Alaric and Genseric, "For
Cassiodorus, who wrote about the year 500 or a little
after it, says, 'The forum of Trajan is a perfect miracle,
if we inspect it even with the utmost minuteness.'"[14]
At a later period the column of Trajan was buried to
the spring of the shaft, and so remained till the time of
Sixtus the Fifth.   That pontiff first excavated the ground
round it, and these works have been at subsequent times
enlarged to the extent of the area of the great Basilica.[15]
A legend of the middle ages commemorating the justice
of Trajan is given in the Purgatorio of Dante, and alluded
to in the Paradise.   Gregory the Great, on a time, passing
through the forum of Trajan noticed a bas-relief that represented that emperor leaving Rome at the head of his
army and stopped by a poor widow, who cried to him for
justice against the murderer of her son.   The emperor was
fain to put her off, but when she reproached him with
neglect of duty he yielded to her importunity.   After
hearing this account of the scene represented, St. Gregory
prayed for his soul, and was told by an angel in a vision
that he must fulfil the debt of justice still due from Trajan
for his sins.   In this way the emperor was delivered and

[14] Burton, Description of Rome, i. 192.   [15] Burton, Antiq. of Rome.

is found by Dante in Paradise.[16]   Dr. Burton is careful to inform his readers that this story has never been put forward as having claims on any of the orthodox belief.[17]

OTHER ARCHITECTURAL AND ENGINEERING WORKS OF THE EMPEROR TRAJAN.

Besides the forum, column, arch, libraries, one for Greek, one for Latin books, and his temple, Trajan added much to the splendour of Rome.   He "prolonged," says Merivale, the series of halls and porticoes which decorated the Campus Martius.   He constructed a theatre in the same quarter, which was remarkable for its circular shape; another *gymnasium* and another *odeum* consecrated to the display of Grecian arts and accomplishments; new *thermæ*, the site of which was near to those of Titus, if indeed they were not actually an extension of the Flavian edifice."[18]   He brought a tenth aqueduct into Rome from the lake Sabatinus, perhaps completed the arch of Titus. He enlarged the new constructions of the Circus Maximus partly destroyed by Nero's fire.

Out of Rome he made, lengthened, or repaired numerous roads.   The Appian way, that along the shores of the Adriatic, from Beneventum to Brundisium, and one in the fourteenth region of Rome itself.   Others were made through his native Spain, besides those I have described in the north of Germany, and in his Dacian conquests. Francke gives the various inscriptions alluding to these works in detail.[19]   He established posts, runners to carry letters, and travelling regulations along all the great roads of the empire.

Besides the bridges over the Danube, Trajan constructed bridges over the Rhine, the Euphrates, the Tigris, the Araxes, the Tagus at Alcantara and Aqua Flavia, and over the Tormus and the Aufidus in Spain.   His baths and aqueducts were placed at numerous cities and stations.   He made the ports of Centum Cellæ (Civita Vecchia), still in use: those of Ostia, Ancona, and of Parentium in Istria.

---

[16] Purg. x. 73, " Quivi era storiata l' alta gloria
        Del Roman prince, lo cui gran valore
        Mosse Gregorio alla sua gran vittoria." and Par. xxi. 13.
   The story is mentioned by Paul the deacon in his life of Gregory the Great.   Dion Cassius relates a similar story of Hadrian, which is said to have been transferred to the account of Trajan.   Lombardi, notes to Dante, *l.c.*

[17] The subject is represented round a picture of the death of the B. Virgin by Simone in the Pinacotheca of Bologna.   Lindsay, iii., 209.

[18] Hist. of the Romans under the Empire, LXIII.

[19] Gesch. Trajans, 577 s. 99.

In the British Museum is a relic of the vessel which perhaps he built and launched as a temporary summer residence on the lake Nemi.[20]

The triumphal arches of Ancona and Beneventum were erected by this emperor. There seems scarcely a dependency of the Roman empire, or an important city within it, in which Trajan did not leave some memorial of his splendour, and to enumerate them completely would be impossible, nor do I propose more than a general account of them in this place.

A second column of shape, design, and proportions very similar to that of Trajan, was erected to Marcus Aurelius Antoninus in the year 174, now standing in the Piazza Colonna in Rome. It is within a fraction of the same height, but the shaft is less tapering, being between seven and eight diameters in height, instead of eight. The sculptures are in higher relief. They represent the war against the Marcomanni.

This account would be incomplete without some notice of an imitation of the column in our own era cast in bronze, erected in Paris and destroyed two years ago.

The column in the Place Vendôme, destroyed in 1871, was designed on the model of that of Antoninus. The height of the whole is 133 feet (according to Murray's handbook 143 feet (?) by 12). There are eagles on the four corners of the cornice. The bas-reliefs represent the principal actions of the campaign of 1805, "depuis le départ des troupes du camp de Boulogne jusqu'à la conclusion de la paix après la battaille d'Austerlitz."[21] The spiral thread that separates the sculptures contains the names and descriptions of the subjects. It was intended to support the statue of Charlemagne, but Napoleon placed his own there instead. In 1831 Napoleon's statue, dressed as a Roman emperor, was replaced by that of him as General Buonaparte, by Seurre. It was again changed to an exact copy of the earlier figure by Napoleon the Third in 1862.

1873. JOHN HUNGERFORD POLLEN.

---

[20] As early as 1485 an ancient ship, believed to have been built by Trajan, was discovered in this lake. C. T. Newton, Guide to the Blacas Collection, B. Mus., p. 35.

[21] Vaugelas, Soixante Vues, &c.

DESCRIPTION OF THE COLUMN.

DESCRIPTION OF THE COLUMN.

The Trajan Column is of the Tuscan order, but with the characteristics both of the Doric and Corinthian orders in the shaft and base, with enrichments on the capital, torus, and other parts. It stands on a pedestal covered with sculpture, of which the cornice and base mouldings are richly decorated, and the pedestal stands on a plain dado.

On the top of the abacus of the capital is a circular pedestal. On the circular dome-shaped summit of the original stood a colossal statue of Trajan holding a sceptre in his left hand, and in his right, it is supposed, a golden ball in which were placed the ashes of that emperor. The pedestal has been heightened and surmounted by a statue of St. Peter.

Round the edge of the abacus was a trellis of gilt bronze. It is replaced by an upright iron railing. A small portion of the shaft of the column is fluted. The rest is ornamented with a spiral band of sculptured bas-reliefs, bordered by an irregular fillet representing rock work, which separates the several compositions of the sculpture from each other.

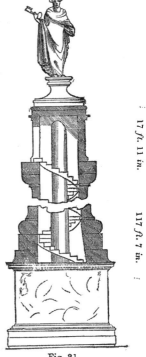

The sculpture begins at once from the apophyges of the lower part and continues to within 18 or 20 inches of the lower members of the capital, leaving room to show the heads of the flutings as stated above. All the surface of the shaft, pedestal, capital, base, &c. have been painted and gilt. On one side of the stylobate is a door giving access to a narrow stair which winds first round the interior of the base and so up the column by a corkscrew stair of 84 steps, each step cut out of the solid marble. It is said that a sepulchral chamber was constructed or proposed beneath the column. The height of the entire structure from the ground to the upper surface of the capital is 117 feet 7 inches. That of the pedestal 17 feet 11 inches, and the statue of Trajan is conjectured to have been

Fig. 31.

17 ft. 11 in.

117 ft. 7 in.

about 20.[22]   The head was found in the débris at the foot
of the column, at the time of the first excavation, and was
taken to the museum of the Cardinal Della Valle.   This
head, which was of bronze, measured two Roman feet
four inches in height.   The marks of the feet were still
visible when the modern pedestal and statue were erected
by Sixtus the fifth.   The subdivisions of the column,
according to the measurement given by Piranesi, which
were found by Messrs. Taylor and Cressy to be correct
in the year 1820, are best seen by the accompanying
woodcut No. 31.   The breadth of the spiral band varies con-
siderably.   Speaking generally it measures two feet in
diameter at the base, and increases to four at the upper
rings; but on being carefully measured in various parts
I found what may be called the same rings of the spiral
varying from three feet to three feet six inches about
one third of the way up the shaft.   This variation depends
on the nature of the different compositions.   The artists
seem to have pushed the dividing line some inches up or
down, wherever the height of objects or the quantity of
detail seemed to require it.   The variation in the width of
the band is so arranged as to preserve an apparent equality
which would be lost altogether, owing to the distance of
the upper portion from the eye, if the true breadth were
uniform from base to summit.

The column could not be seen from any considerable
distance, excepting only the summit, pedestal, and statue of
Trajan visible from the Campus Martius over the tops
of the temples and libraries near it.   It could, however,
be examined from the Greek and Roman Libraries, probably from the upper floors or galleries of the great
Basilica close beside it.   The buildings on the Capitoline and
on the Janiculum must have been close above it, so that,
though now the figures are indistinguishable as the column
stands in its denudation of all accompanying buildings,
they could be easily studied in their original state with
cornices, galleries, and elevated ground on every side.

With regard to the colouring Francke describes the
results of an examination of the under side of the abacus
and various parts of the side of the shaft which show traces
of green, blue, red, and gilding.

In 1833 a committee of artists, under the presidency of
the German architect, M. Semper, examined the column
and attested to the fact that it had been painted, and that

---

[22] The height is considered by Francke to have been about 20 feet, taking
this head as a standard of measurement.

traces of the pigments were still to be traced. Towards the
south, the side furthest from the Capitoline, these traces
have disappeared, that being the quarter from which the
weather beats on it with the greatest severity. On other
sides traces remain of a pigment of yellow colour sometimes
approaching to red, but oftener pure yellow. Under the
abacus the pigment appears to have been little disturbed.
The outer surface has blackened with time, and resembles,
according to the statement of the committee, the remains
yet to be seen on the Temple of Theseus and that of the
Parthenon at Athens. The material is now hard, thick,
and full of bubbles and irregularities, like *old pitch on
the sides of ships*, and it is vitreous at the fractures
whenever it was found possible to chip pieces of it off
without bringing away portions of the marble with them.
The colour seems to have been of a pale green (perhaps
originally blue), with traces also of red. At the neck of the
capital and in the chanellings are distinct remains of blue.
The figures are said by these gentlemen to have been gilt on
a dark ground, the water, trees, buildings, rocks, &c. to
have been coloured appropriately to the subjects represented,
and the wavy line between the rings gilt. It is more
probable that the arms, armour, and accoutrements of the
figures were gilt than that the whole figures were so, as
groups would be less rather than more distinct, unless such
a careful distinction were preserved. The empty spaces
were blue like the flutings, &c. above. The colouring of
the pedestal could not be determined. The abacus, they
thought, had been blue, though they seem to speak of it
above as green. Perhaps the blue had gone from blue to
green in this instance, as in many mediæval wall paintings
executed in encaustic, the vehicle used on the column. On it
they think they traced patterns of some delicate design in
red. The eggs in the mouldings of the capital were green
with gold on it, the hollows blue, the arrows red, and their
edges gilt. Some of these details, according to Francke, want
confirmation; but the main fact of the colouring and the
general prevalence of gold and blue seem to be undoubted.[23]
In such a gorgeous dress the bas-reliefs were at any rate
distinguishable, as they would be if the marble were still
white and transparent, as when it came from the chisel of
Apollodorus and the artists employed under him, instead of
stained with time and weather and battered by arrows,
blows, and cannon shot, as it is at present, from the sieges

[23] See Francke Gesch., p. 188.

the city has undergone and the rude possession taken of it at various times by conquerors of many ages and of all degrees of civilization.

The diameter of the shaft is at the base 12⅛ Roman, not quite 12 English feet, and immediately under the capital this measurement is reduced to 10½ Roman, about 10 English feet. This gives about 7½ diameter, a very elegant proportion.

The exact height of the column was fixed on for a special reason, viz., to show the height of the original spit of hill joining the Quirinal and Capitoline Hills, which was cut away to make room for the forum in which the column is built. A fact commemorated in the inscription on the base. These measurements are those of the original column, and are given in preference to those of the cast in the Museum, which is made up of a number of pieces, no doubt joined with certain inaccuracies, and of which portions may be warped or twisted.

The blocks of which the original column are composed cannot be shown in the cast. The pedestal is formed of nine pieces, of which the cornice and guscio and the dado are single blocks. The cap and base of the column are single blocks. The shaft is composed of 19 drums.

The upper portion of the column above the spiral shows just the heads of the flutings of the column, which are filled, and end with the increase of thickness in the shaft required for the bas-reliefs. The capital is an ovalo cut into egg and tongue of colossal proportions, the astragal below it is cut at intervals into double beads. Above the ovalo is the abacus, which is without ornament.

The pedestal of the statue is round, and stands on a double round offset or base ornamented with mouldings to each part. It is topped by mouldings, and on the upper surface supported the ancient statue of the Emperor Trajan in bronze, holding a lance in his left hand, which was raised, and a golden orb in his right, in which the ashes of the emperor were placed according to a special privilege granted by the Senate, as intramural burial was contrary to the laws of Rome.

The existing statue of St. Peter stands on a modern base, the sides of which are concave with mouldings where it touches the old plinth, a spreading top and an astragal round the centre of the concave sides.

Round the edges of the platform formed by the upper surface of the abacus there is now a plain railing of perpendicular bars.

The base.

The base is composed of a square dado richly sculptured with upper and lower mouldings delicately carved, standing on a double plinth. Above the upper mouldings is placed the proper base of the column itself, the torus, plinth and lower plinth, which expands with a bold and graceful apophyges to meet the fillet that forms the upper member of the moulding of the dado. Sitting above this curve are four Roman eagles, one at each angle of the upper plinth supporting a swag or garland of oak and other emblematic leaves tied with ribands at the corners, and the upper mouldings of the dado are delicately sculptured all over their surfaces. They consist of a carved cymatium and corona, an ovalo carved with egg and tongue ornament, a cyma recta carved with acanthus leaf, and an astragal. In the lower group at the base of the dado, these two mouldings are reversed and there is a fretted torus below. The carving on these members is in slight relief, so as not to break up their surfaces or destroy the outlines of the various curves and their value in the architectural arrangement. The sculptures on the dado are much injured both by time and violence, having been buried for many centuries, besides which parts have been cut away to admit the wall plates of a roof gable. The general arrangement and outlines, however, remain unchanged, though there is partial ruin in many places.

Beginning with the south side in which the door is cut, the sculpture is divided by a horizontal fillet which passes above the frame of the door.

The upper division contains a tablet supported by winged female figures one on each side. They are gracefully inclined forward, stretching diagonally from corner to corner of the square space they fill. They wear the usual women's tunic or ἱμάτιον gathered up at the waistband and falling over so as to form a graceful sinus. Over this garment is a πέπλον, the ends of which flow loose, and a scarf falls over the furthest shoulder. The lines of all these various loose ends of drapery diverge from the outline of the figure with every variety of graceful curve. On the tablet is the inscription:—SENATUS POPULUSQUE ROMANUS IMPERATORI CÆSARI, DIVI NERVÆ FILIO NERVÆ TRAJANO AUGUSTO GERMANICO DACICO, PONTIFICI MAXIMO TRIBUNITIÆ POTESTATIS XVII° (ANNO) IMPERII VI°, CONSULATUS

VII°, AD DECLARANDUM QUANTÆ ALTITUDINIS
MONS ET LOCUS TAN*(tis oper)*IBUS SIT EGESTUS.
The missing letters (TISOPER) are cut away by the chase
made for the wall plates of a roof, and Gruter and
other commentators have supplied the hiatus with other
letters, such as (TIS RUDER) and (TIS E MONT); but
there is not room for more than the letters supplied in
the text, and that reading certainly better completes the
sentence than any of the others suggested.

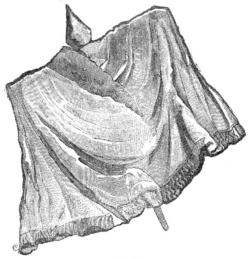

Fig. 32.

The lower half of the sculpture is divided by the doorway which cuts through the plinth and base mouldings, and
gives access by an ascent of three steps to the interior of the
tower. It is framed round by slight lines of moulding.

On the door side the trophy is divided into two parts. That
on the right hand (spectator's left) has on it several Roman
shields, a *sagum*, or military cloak, a *draco*, measuring
25 inches across the bar by 18 inches in depth, including
the fringe; an axe, with one blade and hammer; *lituus*,
the mouth carved into the head of a wolf, with an orna-

mental cresting down the back of the
neck marked off in checquers; a bow
case, pointed casque with a griffin elegantly carved in relief on the side, and
flaps, apparently of fine flexible chain
mail, or leather in this as in similar
casques, on the remaining faces of the

Fig. 33.

stylobate : a *tuba*, straight ; a sword and belt, Roman
3 ft. 8 in. long, with foliated relief
work on the sheath ; part of a
battering ram ; a crooked Dacian
blade, measuring 3 feet, of which
the handle, of wood, with a neck-
ing in the middle, measures

Fig. 34.

$13\frac{1}{2}$ inches ; a coat of plumated or scale mail, the sleeves reaching halfway to the elbow, and part of a corslet of chain mail.

On the other side of the door are several shields ; a *tuba*
and horn or *lituus* wolf headed ; (No. 35) a *draco ;* bow or
arrow case ; *tuba* and a square panel with a boss ornament
much broken, but having an edge of pointed leaves or
rays, perhaps the bow panel of a boat.

Fig. 35.

West side.—Many shields, all slightly varying in ornament,
but several so much alike as to show that they were used
by one particular legion. The first in the lowest row has a
palm on it in low relief. These shields all measure 4 feet
2 in. by 2 ft. 9 in., the measurements varying very little.
Swords of 3 feet, short dirks or *semis-*
pathæ, 2 feet. The hilts are square
blocks, the handles end in a flat pommel ;
the blades measure, with scabbard, 3
inches at the greatest width. On this
side is a linen *lorica* gathered by a narrow
leather strap at the waist in full folds,
and round the neck a *focale* or scarf
tied in two or three places down the

Fig. 36.

chest. Another on the further end of this front is covered
by the *sagum,* or red cloak, fastened by a *fibula* on the
right shoulder and covering the left arm
and back. A Numidian bow on this side
measures 3 feet ; an arrow case with the
arrows 2 ft. 6 in. ; a single arrow on this
side measures 2 ft. 10 in. ; a bow ; a spear,
the head fitted with a socket, length of
the iron head, socket included, 11 inches ;
bow 3 feet (cord) ; helmets with pikes on

Fig. 37.

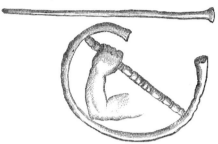

the top; another helmet, circular, high, with cheek pieces, on one of which is a goose in relief; another helmet with a notched crown in relief round the lower edge.

Fig. 38.

North side. — Twenty-six shields with varying ornaments, remains of *pila* and other lances, the shafts of which are all about an inch in diameter, the blade of one of them 8 inches; a *tuba*, a little more than 3 feet long, part being hidden behind a shield; three casques; a *sagum;* an axe 31 inches long, the blade 8 inches wide, and the metal head 8 inches across; a dirk or *semispatha,* of which the blade is 19 inches long by $2\frac{1}{4}$ inches at the widest portion; a Dacian dragon standard. On this front two chases have been rudely cut one under the other, to insert the tiles of a roof.

Fig. 39.

Fig. 40.

East side.—A number of shields; several helmets of Romans and *socii;* a cuirass or shirt of linked chain, the sleeves reaching halfway to the elbow; cuirass of thongs or straps of leather, all buckled down the front of the body. This is the method by which the plate cuirasses of the heavily armed ranks of the Roman legion were fastened together, but the cuirass here shown differs from those worn by the legionaries. Bow and arrow cases similar to those seen attached to the chariots of ancient Egyptian warriors are seen on this front. A Dacian dragon is seen on this front, the body made of linen with spikes or claws at intervals, a head with erect ears, an open mouth, down which the air passed, and inflated the body. The total length is about 6 feet, but there is part of the tail or body rolled up, and the length cannot be ascertained exactly. The head is about 8 inches deep.

Sculptures of the spiral band running up the shaft.

These are numbered as separate scenes or compositions as far as they can be disentangled from the general current of the sculptured story.

I. The first scene represented is the low marsh land of the banks of the Save, a tributary to the Danube. The banks of the river are protected by sentries placed at intervals along the edge of the stream. Four soldiers are represented performing this duty. Two of these are Romans, and two others, according to Bartoli, who gives them beards and bare heads, auxiliaries. But there is nothing in the rest of the military dress to bear out this supposition; probably the second and third heads have worn helmets as well as the first two. The heads are now destroyed. The soldiers wear a cuirass, or thick frock of leather or thick linen, with sleeves to cover the shoulders only, showing the anatomy of the body, and notched in round vandykes over the loins. Under this is a tunic with sleeves halfway to the elbow, and tight drawers reaching halfway down the calf of the leg. They all wear the *sagum*, a cloak or scarf of the shape of the Scotch plaids. This is fastened round the neck by a *fibula*, and falls to the middle of the calf of the leg behind, leaving the right arm, sometimes both, free. This was of wool, and dyed red. On the left arm of each warrior hangs an oval shield about half the length of their bodies, and ornamented with crowns and stars. On their right sides hang swords or daggers. The first two soldiers hold in their right hands, *pila*, but these are only indicated by the action of the hand, as if this weapon was intended for subsequent insertion in metal. As the spears are sometimes represented and at others omitted, and only this action of the right hand is given, this difference represents with more probability the different methods of two artists, amongst the many who have been employed on these bas-reliefs.

The second and third soldiers are occupied in helping the disembarkation of stores from boats, and spears are not given to them. *Focalia* or neckcloths rounds the necks of all these sentries are distinguishable; they pass once round the neck, are tied in a loose slipknot, and the ends hang down in front.

Frœhner [24] considers these men to have belonged to a cohort raised in Narbonnese Gaul.

Each pair of these four men are guards of watch towers or small guard houses, built on piles, such as are now in use on the Austrian frontier. They are represented, however, as structures of stone, are of two stories, the lower lighted only by the door, which can be closed for defence, and the upper by a small square window opening on a wooden gallery with latticed railing to it, on the edge of which leans a large torch of pine wood flaming, as it is night. These small observatories seem to serve as guard houses, having an outer enclosure of stout palisading closely set and the tops of the palisades cut to a point, and also as lighthouses for the navigation of the river at night, and the landing of supplies at all hours.

The guard houses are continued along the shore till lost in the vanishing end of the spiral, diminishing in proportion, but the proportions of the human figure are not altered in this part of the bas-reliefs, so that sentries only occur as soon as the spiral band becomes wide enough to contain these figures.

Between the guard houses are seen stacks of forage brought to a sharp point, and thatched with reeds or rushes of some length, the lengths lapping carefully over each other down to the ground.[25]   Besides corn and hay, firewood is piled up in logs, carefully cut and laid in opposite courses. These logs appear occasionally to have served as beams of timber for various purposes of warlike engineering during the campaign.   The two soldiers employed in landing stores receive them from three small boats or barges, each of the same build.   They are *scaphæ onerariæ* or barges belonging to the boat force kept on the Danube by the Romans under the name of *classis Pannonica*[26] for these purposes.   They are apparently manned by two men each, two men in the first boat are occupied in landing barrels of wine, oil, or vinegar, and perhaps have the other boats also in charge. Each is rowed by two broad paddles, swinging on a thole pin on the quarters of the boat, and a small raised seat is provided in the stern, the planks nailed on by bronze or

---

[24] Description des bas reliefs, Col. Trajane, p. 2.

[25] Columella ii., 18.   " Quiquid siccatum erit, in metas extrui conveniet easque in angustissimos vertices exacui.

[26] Marquardt, Handb. Röm. Alterthum.   Quoted by Frœhner, iii. 2, 407.

copper nails,[27] as being less liable to rust away. This raised seat appears to contain a locker under it.

Two of the boats are laden with casks, and the third with sacks of grain carefully packed and kept in place by bars of timber. A number of the casks are landed, and are lying on an elevated piece of ground.

The artist having thus far represented the military preparations of the emperor changes the scene at once to the rocky banks above the iron gates, from which the campaign is about to open.

The second and third boats are moored abreast of a town, part of which is built on the rocky banks of the river and part on lower ground. This, if a suburb, is carefully fortified by a barricade of palisades pointed at the top and about 10 feet high. The houses have all one upper storey ; the door of one is some height above the ground, and could be reached only by a ladder ; another has the door at the end protected by a small projecting roof or porch, and a third has a long shed on its flank resting on wooden posts ; the roofs of all the buildings are covered with thatch, kept secure by bars of wood, crossed over the entire roof, this arrangement is followed in the more important buildings of the upper town.

This portion is better built. One house has a projecting wing through the basement of which runs a road under an arch. Another building rests on a colonnade of Roman Doric arches, and the upper storey is lighted by square openings or windows. A portion only is seen, and it is a small theatre or forum. Poplar and other trees are seen in an enclosed garden beyond. The town is surrounded by walls built of coursed stones, rusticated, and the tops battlemented for defence. Three arched gates are distinguishable and above them arched openings. Something like what has been preserved over the gate of Augustus at Perugia. From these the warders of the gate could observe the enemy and raise or lower the *cataracta,*[28] *clathra,* or portcullis The principal gateway is arched and has rude pillars each side, and will remind travellers of the Roman arched gateway of Volterra. This arch opens on the quay or landing place of the river, from which a steep road leads to the city: paths or rude stairs in rock lead to the other gates.

---

[27] Vegetius, IV. 34. " Utilius æreis clavibus quam ferreis."
[28] So called because it fell in grooves like a cataract.

The town represents the strong fortification of Vimina-cium, the head quarters of the Claudian legion. It was situated a little to the east of the confluence of the river Morava; it is the modern Ostrava opposite to a narrow island of the same name. From this point the campaign against Decebalus swept to the east and north-east, securing the left bank of the river, and the whole country of Wallachia and Moldavia which lay before Trajan in this direction.

II.—*The Passage of the Danube by the Emperor and his Army.*

The troops march across a bridge laid on boats and carefully engineered. To the left of the bridge under a cave in the rocky shore is a head in relief of heroic size, representing the *numen* of the Danube, a demi figure nude to the elbows, about which a scarf in close folds forms a frame. His back is turned to the spectator, and the head looks to the right in profile. It is a noble face, and is raised as if in anxious concern for the welfare of the emperor. Rivers in antiquity, such as the Tiber and the Nile, are thus personified. The latter deity is finely represented in a marble group in the Vatican. They were supposed to be concerned in all that passed on their streams. Of bridges and dykes they were believed to be jealous, as of bonds or restraints on their own liberty. Trajan, whose religious exactness is fully represented in the course of these bas-reliefs, is careful to show the consent of the Danube god to the erection of his bridge; his right hand is accordingly upholding one of the boats; the thumb of the divinity is shown through the water under the stern of the second boat.

The bridge is constructed in two lengths, taking the island of Ostrava in its course. The boats are seen moored stem on to the stream; broad joists or thick planks set on edge close together appear to be laid across each boat, the ends of which show just before the raised seat or poop in the stern. Across these are laid joists or short timbers, and on these timbers a floor of planks. The sides are protected by strong latticed rails, which also serve as girders to con-nect the different boats, and give additional strength to the platform sufficient to bear infantry, cavalry, stores, and such artillery as Trajan had in use. At the shore end of the bridge, on the Wallachian or left bank where the ground is low, piles have been driven into the bed of the stream, and a steady landing platform or pier constructed, on which the framework of the bridge is made to abut.[29]

The men pass over in double file, the width of the gateway and platforms not admitting of any wider formation. They are headed by their standard bearers and officers, and the emperor is in advance of the entire body.

The soldiers wear a short linen tunic, but only the standard bearers and officers appear to wear drawers in this portion of the bas-relief. They wear light breast and back plates of iron, lobster-scaled shoulder pieces, and similar bands or wide scales or plates of armour round the ribs down to the groin. These plates are tied by leather thongs, and are of bronze, and very light. The only heavy armour is the helmet, a close head-piece with hinged cheek pieces, and a projecting horizontal plate over the forehead, with a socket on the crown for a plume. These helmets are all slung over the shoulders on the march. Besides this, the shield, square at the ends, half cylindrical, is carried on the left arm. A crown and stars decorate the shields of these soldiers. The sword is a straight two-edged cross-handled weapon, with a heavy round pommel on the hilt. Each soldier carries his kit and provisions on a forked staff over the left shoulder, and grasps the *pilum* or short spear in his right.

Fig. 41.

Each man has a small pack or bag crossed diagonally by double straps ; a small goatskin full of wine or vinegar ; a net to hold fruit, meat, or fresh bread ; a ladle for dipping into water and for a drinking vessel ; and a pot or stewpan with an upright handle.[30] They are shod with sandals.

In front of the column march the standard bearers, *vexilliferi.* The standards are of several descriptions. Two

---

[29] Vegetius notes this, a principle always adopted in military bridges across rapid rivers. Lib. I., 37.

[30] See its use, No. LXXXIII.

H

of these are ensigns of *manipuli.* These standards bear a
hand, one is open, the other closed. Round the hands are
wreaths. The hands are on cross bars, ending in trefoil
ornaments, with short streamers hanging from them. Six
pateræ or plates, with bosses in their centres, are fastened
to the staff; below these they bear a crescent and wreath,
in honour of victory.

The standards of the cohorts are the *dracones,* small
banners of cloth fastened to a horizontal bar, the centre of
which hangs on the staff of the ensign. Other standards
have metal forks, *pateræ,* places for inscriptions, busts of
the emperors from whom they had their names. At the
base of these various ornaments is a half circle or globe
with a wreath of leaves in relief around it. On the top
of the standards is a figure, one of victory, with palm and
crown, or of another divinity. One appears to be Mars as
he holds a naked sword.

The bearers, *signiferi, imaginiferi, draconarii,* wear the
skins of bears over their shoulders; the skin of the animal's
face serving as a protection to the wearer's head, in place
of a helmet.

Two *aquiliferi* are seen crossing the Danube. The staves
or poles of the standard are topped by a square bracket or
stand ornamented with a cornice on its under side. The
wings of one eagle are coupled or united at their extremities by a mural crown in the honour of former achievements of the legion. The other standard is without the
eagle, and probably represents that lost by Cornelius Fuscus
under Domitian, and which was recovered by Trajan.

There are two superior officers, tribunes, marching at
the head of the men. They wear armour to the waist,
and kilts or skirts of thongs of leather, which are girt
round the waist, the points hanging in two rows round the
loins; similar pieces fall over the shoulders; the arms are
bare; the legs are clothed in tight hose that covers the
legs to the middle of the calf, and the feet in sandals
bound with straps round the ancles; their heads are bare;
they carry a short straight sword only in a metal scabbard
belted round the waist, and hanging at the left side;
they carry in the right hand a roll of paper or a short
baton, and a cloak clasped over the right shoulder.

Two trumpeters, *cornicenes,* are sounding the signal for
the march. Their instruments are large semicircular horns
of brass connected by a straight bar, on the ends of which
is a semicircular plate like the blade of an axe. They are
here giving the signal for the advance over the bridge. At

the head of the entire advanced guard marches the emperor Trajan himself. He is dressed like his lieutenants, wears a cloak clasped over his shoulder, and gives the signal of the advance with his left hand.

The leaves on the trees indicate that the summer has begun. The emperor has a horse led before him. The horse is without saddle, but is covered by a saddle cloth fastened round him with a surcingle, and kept in place by a breastplate strap and a similar strap over the loins, from which hang trefoil ornaments of gilt bronze ; the cloth is vandyked on the edge, perhaps with gold embroidery. There are no indications of stirrups. There is an upper cloth, the lower of the two is fringed with gold. The head is without ornament. The headstall consists of a cheek strap, throat lash, forehead strap, and a nose band, and the sharp bit has long bars. It is ornamented with rosettes or bosses of bronze gilt, and so are all the junctions of straps in the harness.

Trajan never rode on a march, but had his horse led before him.

A band of eleven young men and five horses are close to the emperor's person, and are officers selected to fill the place of aides-de-camp, and carry orders to and fro. The horses have oval shields hung on the sides of the saddles.

III.—*Council of war.*

The first act of Trajan after landing on the Wallachian shore is to hold a council of war. The emperor, the prefect of the prætorians, and another of his lieutenants, are seated on a *suggestum*, a platform represented by square lines, probably not stones, which could not be put together for so temporary an occasion, but square turfs erected breast height, as we see by the standard bearers and representatives of various arms of the legion round it. This bank is large enough to hold the curule seat of the emperor and of his next in command, and the third is accommodated with a seat of turf. There is room also for eight *lictors* with *fasces* that stand round the group. The *lictors* are dressed in the tunic, and the toga or cloak is drawn over the shoulders and arms, and tied in a knot below the neck, the ends falling down. More than one of the soldiers wear a *focale* or neckcloth loosely tied in front. The Romans seem to protect themselves by these means from the climate of Wallachia. The emperor is turning to ask the advice or give his instructions to his lieutenants, but the head of the figure is gone ; the action of the hands and of the legs are vigorously rendered, and fully express the artist's meaning.

The horses of the emperor are hurried forward, and two *dracones* or cohort ensigns are carried along with them. A cannon shot has broken out a round hole in this part of the column, fortunately in the wall of the platform under the seats of the council.

IV.—*First sacrifice.*

Trajan before beginning the campaign against the Dacians offers the sacrifice of the *Suovetaurilia.* In the background is a fortified camp surrounded by trees. It is not square but round or semicircular. The outer enclosure is of square blocks of turf built regularly, as if with hewn stones, and battlements, or square *pinnæ* are left at intervals to protect the sentries. There are five tents, *papiliones,* made of skins, cloth, linen, or wool, decorated with fringed valances cut into large notches, and the entrances protected by ample curtains. The outsides are protected by cords crossed and tied in large reticulations over the roofs and sides, against the danger of being carried away by the weather. In front of the imperial tent are ranged the standards of the legions. On the extreme left of the enclosed space one eagle is between two of the ensigns already described as those of the *manipuli.* An eagle enclosed within a circular wreath, with the wings half open, forms the top ornament of these two standards. At the back of the eagle is a *draco ;* to the right of these is a group of three more standards, the ornaments being a thick horizontal wreath of leaf work above a semi-globular ornament also of leaf work. Above the wreath is a bust of one of the emperors in a large wreathed medallion, then another horizontal wreath above that, which seems to be an eagle in a medallion, then another horizontal wreath and on the top a globe, or what looks like it, but this part is much decayed. There are three of these standards and all have suffered alike as regards the top ornament, so that it is not possible to state exactly what these ornaments were.

Before the prætorian or principal entrance to the parade in front of the tents a small altar, of square stones, has been erected. It is about three feet in height by 18 inches or so in breadth on each face. On this the emperor, as the *Pontifex Maximus* is offering a sacrifice. He is arrayed in white linen and wears the toga in the fashion called *cinctus*

Gabinus, a portion covering the head like a veil. This mantle covers him almost to the feet which are clothed in white boots bound round the ancles. In his left hand is the *lituus,* a short staff curling over on the end. His right hand holds a *patera,* and from this he is pouring a libation on the fire that burns upon the altar. His face expresses the utmost solemnity.

In front of him is a *camillus.* He holds a vase from which wine has been poured into the dish already mentioned. On the right of the emperor a *tibicen* or flute player is performing on a double flute such a religious melody as may soothe the hearers, keep them silent, and prevent as far as possible anything in the nature of a sound, even a breath out of harmony with the sacred occupation. Two attendants, attired like the sacrificer in white togas, stand on each side and appear to be looking anxiously around to ensure silence. In front of these personages, and partly screened from them by the outer dyke or wall of the camp, are the other attendants who take part in the ceremony. To the right is the *cultrarius,* stripped to the waist and clothed with the *limus,* an ample skirt descending to the feet on which are sandals ; buckled round his waist hangs a leather case on the right hip, in which are two small knives, *cultra,* from the use of which in cutting the throats of the victims this official took his name. To his left is the *popa,* also stripped to the waist and bearing a poleaxe, one side of the blade sharp and the other in the form of a square hammer. His office was to fell the victim with a blow on the brain. In front of him is a bull with the *dorsale,* a narrow cloth like a stole, fringed with gold hanging over its back and reaching halfway down the flank. Further on are two *victimarii* holding a ram that tries to escape and a pig. Behind the *cultrarius* is an attendant holding what has been a vase of lustral or purifying water, with which the victims and attendants are to be sprinkled. Behind him a man holds up on high a small dish containing what looks like a cucumber or a cake, to represent the first fruits of the earth. A crowd of attendants is standing round. All are crowned with leaves or with a ribbon bound round the head.

V.—*Trajan breaks up his camp.*

The emperor, with his two lieutenants, is standing on a raised platform such as has been already described. It appears to be the back of one from which he is seen in the next composition making the traditional speech to his troops. He gives a signal with his hand, which is obeyed by the trumpets of the legions. Six trumpeters, some with the *tuba,* a long straight trumpet of brass, and others with the *cornu,* the curved brass horn already described are sounding for the break up of the camp. Before this rear end of the platform is seen a slave falling from his mule. This scene has been strangely interpreted by commentators. Muziano, the painter, who first made a series of drawings from the column in the sixteenth century, seems to have offered no opinion on the meaning of this composition, nor does Bartoli who follows him. Froehner suggests that it may represent the ambassador from the Burri, that he falls terrified from his mule at the sudden appearance of the emperor·on a hill. Dion Cassius related a somewhat similar story. The message sent to Trajan was written on the surface or head of a mushroom, and the circular pierced plate represented on the mule's back is suggested as an explanation. But it is impossible, with the cast of the actual sculpture before us, to accept of such an interpretation. A messenger from a people able to send terms or exhortations in writing would not be unaccompanied, nor would he be alone in the Roman lines without guards to admit and introduce him to the emperor. In the composition here described the man is alone, dressed in the frock or tunic of a slave only, of whom numbers were carried with the Roman armies as camp followers.

The incident is simply the fall of a scullion from his mule, which is startled by the sound of the various signals given so near, and has kicked him off. He holds not a mushroom of any kind but a round kitchen drainer pierced with holes made by the drill, a tool generally used by the sculptors of these bas-reliefs. The action of the ears of the mule, even a wicked look in its eye, are rendered by the sculptor, who is singularly faithful in his portraiture of animals wherever they occur.

A window is formed above the back of the mule, which it touches, to give light to the staircase within.

VI.—*Trajan addresses his troops.*

Following the immemorial custom of ancient generals and leaders Trajan is here addressing his troops. Men representing various arms of the legion, standard bearers, and others are crowded to listen. · Three out of five men in the front whose backs are turned to the spectator wear the cuirass made of thin plates of metal rivetted together and reaching to the loins only ; the others wear linen cuirasses. All have helmets. The shields are of two shapes, curved with square ends, or oval, ornamented some with stars and crescents, some with the arms of Jove. The emperor stands on the front of the tribunal described above. The same two officers, who are seen supporting him while giving the signal to break up his camp, are here in a like position. This structure has been prepared for the purpose, and it is from the back of it that Trajan, who has received the last intelligence or advice offered by his lieutenants, gives the signal for putting his army into motion.

VII.—*Construction of a fortified camp.*

The constructions undertaken in this composition are of a kind more durable than those required for an entrenched camp only, as in the last instance of such a work. Not only are hewn stones used, but there is a triple line of walls. This was in accordance with the most advanced theories of Roman fortification. Each line of walls, it will be observed, is higher than that which is in its front. This was arranged with the object, not only of discharging missiles with safety over the heads of the defenders in front, but to prevent the near approach of hostile engines, whether towers or battering rams, by the circles of wet ditches interposed between the lines of wall. The slot or channel down which it is intended that the *cataphracta*, portcullis, shall be dropped is shown in the centre of one of the walls. Only one side is shown, which was all that was required by the artist to make his meaning clear. The gate itself, with the passages closed by this engine and by doors, is still to be constructed, and may be meant to run some way along the wall, as in those of the entrances to the fortified towns of Conway, and other instances of mediæval military engineering, both in this country and on the continent of Europe, thereby obliging besiegers to attack the gate itself at great disadvantage. A soldier is half seen working at the foundation of the outer walls. He hands a round flat-bottomed basket without handles, *cophinus*, to his fellow. Another lifts a stone of considerable weight from a scaffold, or from a heap of stones, to a soldier doing some mason's work on the second wall. The action of the back and shoulder is seen as he accommodates himself to land his burden on the wall. The same is going on in other parts. The workmen are all fighting men, and work in their breast and shoulder

armour. The shields and helmets are laid aside. Two
are seen, the helmet on the spear head, the shaft being
struck into the ground, and the shield is leaning against it.
Two sentries stand by in cuirasses and indicating by the
raised action of the arm, and the grasp of the hand that
they are holding spears, which are not given by the sculptor.

No buildings are visible inside this enclosure, as in some
other fortified towns met with in other parts of the
sculpture, only tents. The top of the walls, where finished,
are ornamented with a moulding of beads or round plates
or show the ends of timber beams required for wooden
galleries for purposes of defence.

VIII.— *Additional fortified station.*

Beyond a small river or stream across which this fortification is astride is seen another fort, or another portion
of the same. They are joined by a bridge of timber. The
bridge consists of two strong latticed girders, the lower
member of which sustains stout planks that form the road
itself. The girders are supported by piers composed of
piles with struts on either side, driven at intervals into the
bed of the river, the planks are carefully shown in a perspective projection. The distance between these fortifications
is not large. A soldier is seen carrying a large beam to
be driven as a pile into the river to complete the bridge.
Another hammers a chisel into the top of one of the piers,
to prepare it to be morticed into the top rail. A heavy
beam is carried up to this second fortification by two soldiers. It has two walls or enclosures, the lower wall partly
finished in the same way as the last described In front of
this is a soldier half hidden in the ground digging the outer
fosse, and a figure is giving him directions and preparing to
receive from him a basket of sand and gravel. A gateway
is left in this lower wall. Three shields square on the
ends are standing with helmets on lances stuck in the
ground belonging to the working parties, and three sentries,
their shields resting on the ground and lances gripped in
their right hands (but not given) keep guard. Beside
them is the bearskin head-piece of a standard bearer.
Above the low wall is seen Trajan and his two generals in-
,specting and giving directions. There are trees within the
walls, and the tents or *papiliones* can be distinguished as
well.

A third enclosure is fortified by a separate wall of hewn
stone. It is circular. Soldiers are at work on all sides of

it. One carries a heavy stone on frame consisting of a pair
of staves, one over each shoulder, united into a hod on the
shoulders. He lodges the stone with his back against the
wall in the hands of one of the masons. Another is sitting
and receives a squared stone, which is lifted up to him.
Two *papiliones* are already pitched within this enclosure.
A beam is being carried to the top of the back wall; a
soldier is using the adze, and between these can be distinguished the helmet of one of the men, upright on a spear
head.

Above these three enclosures is an *arx* or donjon, to
which there is a bridge leading from the circular fort,
probably crossing an arm of the stream already mentioned.
A rocky path from the outside leads also to this building. It has three towers which project in a semicircle
from the circuit of the walls. A door is also finished, but
it is not yet guarded. Several wooden galleries can be distinguished over the parapets of the towers and the platform
above the gates.

Another bridge connects the round fortification with the
open country, from which it is separated by a stream, the
same that probably runs between the upper citadel and
this position. Over the bridge three spies, *exploratores*,
careful men selected for the purpose, are sent forward by
the emperor to reconnoitre the enemy. They wear linen
cuirasses only, so as to have as little as possible to hamper the
activity of their movements, and are armed with the short
pilum, which can be made out by the vigorous action of
their hands; they have oval shields. They are runners.
A soldier on the far side of the fosse dips a kettle or
handled pot into the river to draw water.

IX.—*A wood.*

The nature of the country explains the necessity of
carefully feeling for the enemy and ascertaining his strength.
The army is in a dense forest traversed, as we have seen, by
rocky streams.

The legionaries are employed in clearing the wood.
Three are cutting down trees with axes. Two carry a log
of large scantling slung by a stout rope in the centre to
a bar or pole, one end resting on the shoulders of each.
Another with both arms is lifting a large piece of timber.
This is preparatory to the erection of another fortified position. A small bridge is laid over a stream in this part.
They are evidently constructing well laid roads through the
country as they advance.

X.—*Another Fortified Position.*

This fortification appears to be built close above the Danube, or one of its larger tributaries. A tree divides the operations of the builders from the forest last described. On a hill may be seen through the boughs of this tree a mule with a Spanish saddle, with a broad ledge hung from it, on which the rider sits sideways and can support both feet so as to enable him to study papers or plans placed on his knees while riding. The mule is held by a slave.

The fort, like the last, consists of separate enclosures within the largest. One block to the left of the composition is separately surrounded and fortified. Soldiers are busy about this portion constructing various wooden frames for portcullises, catapults, palisades, &c.

The outer wall appears to be built in zigzags, so as to give the defenders the command of the various faces, as well as to follow the inequalities of the rocky bank or heights on which the place is built. A workman is seen on the right, who appears by the rammer he is using to be ramming down concrete in a wall of great thickness, the faces only of which are of hewn stone. This is the more probable as we observe in several of these building scenes the prominence given to sand and gravel, which is handed in baskets to the builders. Another soldier, with a large beam of wood, is kneeling and listening to Trajan, who, with two officers, is inspecting the works in the foreground and giving directions.

Sentries mount guard in the re-entering angles of the walls. Trees are retained within the walls, and tents are distinguishable beyond them. To the left two soldiers carry another heavy beam. Below the main walls an enclosure of palisades set close together, with pointed tops, to protect meadow land and rickyards. Two ricks thatched with rushes are seen over the palisades, and a small pier supported on tripod piles driven into the river is constructed for facilitating the embarcation, and for discharging barge loads of hay and provisions. The water is seen to come right up to the palisades.

A separate building with walls and round towers stands on an eminence to the left in advance of the other works, before the door of which are prætorian guards standing sentry. This building is further from the river.

XI.—*A prisoner.*

Beyond these, in advance, to the left (spectator's right) Trajan, with a numerous bodyguard behind him, receives two Dacian prisoners. They are bearded men dressed in linen tunics and loose trowsers, which are tied round the ankles and shoes. They wear no headdress. Over their shoulders is a short cloak, *sagum*. The features of the nearest are dignified, the nose prominent and hooked, and the general character appears to show vigour and sagacity. This character is expressed by the sculptors more or less throughout these bas-reliefs where Dacian warriors are introduced.

A soldier drives these men with great violence to the emperor's presence. He thrusts one man forward by the hair at the back of his head. The arms of the prisoners are bound behind them. Trajan appears to be examining these men. His right hand is across his body, and he turns to his lieutenants to hear or ask their opinion.

XII.—*Construction of a bridge.*

A bridge is being thrown over what is probably an affluent of the Danube, and lies across the great military road which the emperor is constructing. Five soldiers are occupied, lifting, fitting, and nailing together timbers for this bridge. It is supported on latticed girders strengthened by piles driven into the bed of the river. Several men, with mallet and chisel, are shaping different portions of the bridge. One drives a rough pile into the bed of the river, two more bear a heavy beam to complete the top of one of the girders. The timber has been carefully squared. One of the uprights of the girders is completed with a moulded abacus at the point of junction with the beam that rests on it.

XIII.—*Fortified camp or oppidum.*

A fortified post is being constructed with the same care, and the work pushed on with the same activity as the last. A man lifts a heavy stone to another on the walls. A mason sits and receives a heavy stone, on what seems to be an intermediate wall just begun, and intended as a third line or circumvallation, or for the foundation of a building of solid stone to be raised within it. A heavy stone is borne by two soldiers on a shoulder hod formed by two boughs one over each shoulder, or the two ends of a rope strained tight by the weight of the stone it holds.

In front men are digging and preparing to fortify an outwork. This outwork, from the cavity in which they work and from which baskets of sand and shingle are being lifted, appears to be intended for a small basin or harbour, such as will be seen completed in other bas-reliefs representing river side forts and towns. This basin is being surrounded by walls of hewn masonry which appear just above the ground, and it is separated from the river only by a narrow space of ground through which probably it is intended to cut an opening when the arch is completed. This fortress communicates with the lower ground, along which the road is carried by a bridge constructed like those already described. The side walls are seen following the edge of a precipitous side of the rocky eminence on which the fort is built, and sentries at intervals are standing on the edge of the cliff outside, so as to command a view of the open country. Higher up is a small enclosed citadel with walls, oval or circular, and semicircular towers at intervals, and an arched gateway. But this is not yet guarded by sentries. The emperor is looking on.

The horses of the emperor.

Though the Emperor Trajan rarely rode on the march, but shared the fatigues of his troops, he is followed by led horses in more than one of these compositions. Five horses held by five attendants (who, from their linen cuirasses, are intended for legionaries, but who are unarmed,) are waiting behind the fortifications, for which a soldier is seen hewing down a tree. They appear to be kept ready for the emperor to ride round and inspect the various engineering works that are going on.

XIV.—*The emperor sends out mounted spies.*

From the lower left (spectator's right) angle of this town the emperor is sending out a mounted party of three explorers to reconnoitre. Their horses have saddlecloths, ornamental straps at intervals over the mane and round the neck. They carry oval shields and appear to grasp their drawn swords. The emperor is giving them their final instructions. These men are picked from a sort of staff selected from the best men of the legion.

At a distance can be distinguished a mountain fort. It appears to be small. The walls are carefully constructed, and the gate is deeply recessed between two towers. Inside are three buildings of solid masonry, one long building with a roof of one slope. Another has a door at the end, and a chamber with a square window over it. Wooden structures are raised within the walls with railed platforms upon them to serve as observatories. These are meant by the artist to be represented as built on mounds or heights within the place.

XV.—*General advance of the Roman army.*

The reconnoitring party does not return, but the enemy is known to be close at hand, and an advance is ordered of the whole Roman army. It is still a thickly wooded country, and a working party is employed in clearing a road for the legions. Three men are employed removing the trees with all haste. Two use axes (which are not sculptured), and a third is pulling the head of the tree to hasten its fall. Three other men are trying to pull a tree down, which there is no time to cut with axes. A soldier has already cut one down, and secures the log for future use, while the stump of the tree is shown. Further in advance is seen a part of the rear guard of the army. With the body are the standards of one of the legions. An *aquilifer* carries an eagle between two standards of *manipuli*. Both the bearers of these standards carry them resting against the left shoulder and with their right hand seem to prop or push them upright, as if to push through overhanging boughs and other impediments. All three wear cloaks clasped in front, linen cuirasses, bearskin head-pieces, but neither shields nor arms. The *aquilifer* has nothing on his head. A man is seen in profile in advance of the standards, apparently watching what goes forward in the front. The shield of one of the workmen is lying on the ground, not propped in the usual way, showing the pressure under which the legions are hurried to the front. All the legionaries forming this body wear the square sided shield.

Further on, with the main body of the Roman army, are distinguished five standards of *manipuli*. These men are drawn up waiting for orders. Two standards have hands on their tops, two have eagles surrounded by wreaths, and one has among the ornaments near the base the gate or front of a town. These differences enabled the men of different subdivisions of the legion to find their places in the ranks during the movement or confusion of general actions. The title of each legion is under or round the imperial bust, where these are seen, but that is not the case with every one of these standards in the legion.

XVI.—*First battle.*

In the first encounter with the enemy the attack appears to be made by the Dacians. It is sustained with great vigour. They employ infantry only. Two men lie dead in advance, and a third is fighting hand to hand with a Roman horseman. There are other Dacians behind engaged with the light-armed Roman infantry. The Dacians are seen, cutting *cæsim*, with their swords, which are straight and short, though longer than those of the Romans. Their shields are oval, flat, ornamented with two stars or flowers and a central boss. They are draped in linen drawers and tunics, wear shoes, and fringed cloaks, *saga*, which are pinned with brooches over each shoulder, the cloak passing under one arm and leaving both arms free. They have no covering of any kind for the head, which is well clothed with thick curling hair. A wounded Dacian, half lying, is about to be despatched by the club of a man nude, all but a cincture round the loins. He belongs to a body of German auxiliaries, who, according to Tacitus, fought so attired.

A Roman soldier beyond these combatants is fighting with a human head held by the hair between his teeth. The head is to be shown as a trophy, and to entitle the bearer to special allowances of corn. The Roman soldiers gain ground in the back of the composition. The Dacians have a number of archers in that part of the battle. Their bows are short, but of great thickness, curved like the classic bow. They carry their arrows in a round case or quiver that hangs over the left shoulder. The distinct character of the heads on the two sides is well preserved. In the rear of the Dacian army are seen wounded and dead men. A young man, badly hurt, is carried tenderly by two older men; another lies in the foreground, his left hand still supported on his shield, which he tries to retain to the last; a third is in the act of falling to the ground.

They have two standards, one a *labarum* or *draco*, such as was used by the Roman cohorts, perhaps a trophy taken by the Dacians, and the other a Dacian dragon. The head is towards the Romans, indicating that it is still in the possession of the enemy.

A body of Dacians is still in reserve or not yet engaged. In the rear of the Romans, Trajan and his lieutenants are watching and directing the battle. The Romans, besides the infantry described, employ cavalry. Three horsemen are shown by the artist charging sword in hand. Two infantry soldiers hold up heads in their hands to attract the notice of the emperor.

There is another round fortified camp to which Trajan
has his back, and from the eminence on which it is constructed he is able to command the field of battle.

On the Roman side Jupiter is represented looking on
and taking part in the struggle. A venerable bearded
figure is seen to the waist encompassed by clouds above,
and by a stream of water, represented by wavy lines below.
He looks indignantly to the Dacians, and the right arm is
stretched in the act of hurling his thunderbolts at the
enemy. In the Autonine column a similar composition
represents *Jupiter Pluvius* overwhelming the enemies of
the empire with rain and snow. In the present instance,
the deity may be supposed to commemorate a thunder-
storm occurring during the action. The Dacians wear shoes.
Their swords are sometimes straight, a little longer than
those of the Roman legionaries, and look as though many
had been spoils of the wars under Domitian, and were
of Roman make. Their shields are oval, and differ from
the oval shields of the Romans in having other ornaments upon them. One Dacian leader wears what looks
like a woollen cap fitting the head, but high and loose
enough to ruck up into creases when drawn on to the head;
another, a handkerchief bound round his head; otherwise
their heads are unprotected. They have close and thick
hair. The battle is fought on forest ground, and a log or
portion of a tree trunk is left on the ground in front of
the Roman cavalry apparently as an impediment to their
movements.

XVII.—*Burning of the Dacian quarters.*

The emperor, holding a spear, has ascended a rocky
eminence. In two or three places before and behind him,
apparently in his path, are short and low walls, on the face
of which are upright ribs. Some interpret these as ramps
of a staircase.[31] They are more like impediments to the
ascent of the path. Before him are small square enclosures
formed by stone copings, in which are pairs of small obelisks
or *cippi*, or memorial stones, which Muziano considers to
be Dacian graves. These are outside a double wall, protected by a wet ditch, forming a semicircle, part of the
enclosure of a fortified place. The wall is of masonry. It
is entered by an arched gateway, covered by a lofty pediment, and approached by a wooden bridge, removable,

---

[31] Frœhner, Col. Traj.

though not hung by chains.   On the far side of the double wall is a row of six heads on spears.   They are wasted almost to skeletons, are beardless, and probably represent Roman captives taken in the wars of Domitian.   A standard, a Roman *draco* with fringed edge, is struck up amongst them, on it can be distinguished the letter R.   Two wooden look-out structures are erected on the same spot. One is a small square guard house showing a square window in the front, a gabled roof, and a circular opening in the gable.   It stands on four posts.   The other is round, of large size, open at the top, and defended by a bulwark of stout upright planks set close together, and pointed on the tops.   Beside this is a Dacian serpent standard also fixed upright in the ground.

Beyond these look-outs are two roofed buildings of masonry.   Trajan is giving orders to set the whole place on fire.   In the foreground below the rock on which he stands are Dacian houses of wood.   One is on posts, covered and roofed with planking and skins, in which the nails can be distinguished. The planking is strengthened by outside beams nailed across them.   There is a square window on the end, and the roof is gabled.   It is entered by a ladder.   Another wooden building, similarly constructed, is built on the ground, and entered by a door on the ground floor.   They are defended by an enclosure of palisades set close together and pointed.   Soldiers are setting fire to these buildings. The whole fortress has the appearance of a Roman station occupied by the enemy, who have added wooden buildings to the stone erections of the former possessors.   A square fort is seen in the distance.   The beaten army retreats through the dense forest.

XVIII.—*Passage of a river.*

The Roman army is pushed forward to complete the rout of the enemy and cross the river (Tjerna?) at a ford. The banks are wooded.   The legionaries headed by their *signiferi* are dashing across the river.   Two *signiferi* lead bearing the standard of the *manipuli*.   One steadies the upper part of the standard, which is raised above the head with his right hand.   Both have oval shields, but no side arms.   The emperor, followed immediately by the *aquilifer* bearing the staff of the lost eagle, has gained the opposite bank first, and awaits the passage of the legion.   One soldier is stripped and carries all his arms and accoutrements in the hollow of his shield, which is held by both arms above his head. He wades through water up to his waist.[32] Two *cornicines* are sounding from the further side. On a rock above the ford is a small fort, on the top of which is a wooden platform supported on massive timbers carried up from the outside.

XIX.—*Trajan receives a deputation from the enemy.*

The emperor is seated on a lofty *suggestum.* He is on a chair surrounded by Lucius Quietus and his lieutenants, and by guards and standard bearers, a rampart or wall is erected in front, so as to enclose this elevation, leaving an opening for the admission of the ambassadors. Near the enclosure is the Prætorian camp. Over the top of the rampart are to be seen the tent of the emperor and two sentries on guard.

Between the two enclosures the ambassadors are introduced. Three are mounted, the others are on foot. The horses have saddleclothes, bridles, and headstalls, and the bridles are of chain. Those on foot have shields. One of the horsemen is turning with a look of anger to another body come to parley. The others hold out their hands appealing to the clemency of the emperor, who, to judge from the sequel, seems to exact severe conditions. He holds a lance in his left hand.

XX.—*Reception of another embassy.*

The emperor, with three officers, receives this party standing. He holds his swordbelt in his left hand. They are five, and are all on foot. They are perhaps representatives of an independent tribe forced into rebellion by the Dacians. They wear long fringed cloaks buckled over the right shoulder gathered in the left hand, and tight tunics. There would be no apparent connexion between these two receptions as the emperor is twice represented, but for the action of one of the horsemen described in the last composition.

XXI.—*Flight of the remains of the Dacian force, and destruction of a stronghold.*

In the lower part, in the foreground, are Roman soldiers who have tracked a number of refugees to a hiding place. The Dacians defend themselves, several are wounded. One,

---

[32] Owing to the weight he carried the Roman soldier seldom could swim, Tacitus, v. 14.

a young man, half rising from the ground, defends himself with a club. An old man tries to escape with a child. The place they are in is a cavern or recess under an overhanging cliff. Further on is a cavern in which are cattle of all kinds, concealed there in the first instance, and then slaughtered to avoid their falling into the hands of the Romans.

Along the rock above are three horsemen, armed with clubs, auxiliaries of the legions, or holding lighted torches, as Muziano supposes, and riding to buildings which they are to fire. The rest of the army come up with the fugitives and penetrate a stronghold, in which the old, the women, and children of the enemy have taken refuge. The women carry their infants with them in the effort to escape. A soldier seizes one by the arm. The emperor is seen on a height above. He is giving assurance of protection to the women and children. The houses and buildings are fired. Some of the houses are of wood, and some of stone. The women are draped in ample sleeved gowns, gathered in at the waist. They wear veils on their heads. The hair is plaited round the back of their heads.

XXII.—*Disasters of the Dacian cavalry.*

A number of horsemen are struggling in the water. These are, perhaps, Dacian cavalry attempting an attack on a distant Roman fort during winter time over ice. The ice is insufficient to bear them, and they are seen struggling on the surface of the stream. One man has lost his shield. Two others up to their knees in water have recovered it. Friends on the bank give what help they can to the swimmers. Several horsemen unable to keep their seats are calling for help, and some are drowned, others scramble to the bank as best they can. Along the bank is a line of men mounted and on foot flying in confusion. Three of these horsemen are completely covered with scale armour. Not only the riders, but the horses are so protected. The heads, ears, and legs of the horses are completely covered, as well as the bodies, limbs, and feet of the men, even the eyes of the horses have a thin grating as a protection. This armour was called feathered *plumata*, from the overlapping of the small plates. The heads of the riders are protected by conical head-pieces with cheek plates, but their faces and hands are bare. Two standards, one a *labarum* or *draco* and one the Dacian dragon, are hurried along by the fugitives.

XXIII.—*Assault of a Roman Fort.*

A small detached Roman post is attacked by another portion of this force. The place is circular. It is surrounded by a wall of masonry. There are raised battlements or *pinnæ* of the height of some feet, each having two-arched openings or loop holes at intervals. Between these are small battlements representing the height of one of the courses of masonry. A one-arched gateway is closed by doors, of which a transom at the springing of the arch and an upright bar down the centre can be distinguished. The Romans defend themselves manfully. They are half seen above the battlements, grasp long *pila* and spears in their hands, with which they strike down with all their might on the heads and shields of the assaulting party. They represent all the arms comprised in the legion, and of more than one legion. All these shields are oval ; the ornaments on them are of seven different patterns, two are thunder-bolts of different shapes, one set winged and with stars.

The Dacians attack the walls with great resolution. They are nearly as tall as the walls, but this is a device of the sculptor to bring his subject together, as the doorway half the height of the walls gives their real scale.

Many Dacians are shooting with bows, here disproportionally small. Three men bear a small battering ram, a beam of wood with a ram's head of metal on the end, with which they batter a part of the wall. Those armed with swords and defending themselves with shields await the result, and a favourable chance of mounting a breach. The whole scene is very animated, and as no breach is made we are left to conclude that the enemy is forced to raise the siege and retire.

XXIV.—*Preparation for a fresh campaign.*

The head-quarters of the Roman army are fixed in a town well built, and made the seat of a Roman colony. It is surrounded by walls, and has a defensible post in the river, which is entered by an arch, which has something of the character of those erected by the emperor at Ancona and Beneventum. An open place or forum is surrounded by buildings of no great architectural pretension, but still carefully constructed, and having the characteristics of Roman civil architecture. One has a colonnade of these arches in front. The town gate is under a lofty arch, such as the gate of Augustus at Perugia, and an amphitheatre is carefully sculptured. It stands on arches, as does that of Nismes, and has a row of square windows round the periphery of the upper corridor, which may be supposed to give access to the higher benches. Rows of seats down to the ground can be distinguished over the top, as the artist has shown this in a perspective method. This portion of the town appears to be external to the rest, or to occupy a height which, without being detached, may form a separate quarter.

Immense activity is shown in the landing of stores and other preparations in this place for an immediate advance, probably for a second passage of the Danube by a separate portion of the Roman army. Convoys of large transport boats are seen bringing stores of all kinds, which are landed by soldiers of the garrison. Besides corn the first vessel carries stores of arms, shields, and armour. The boats are protected by liburnians, light vessels of war, carrying two or three banks of oars. Sacks of grain are seen corded carefully over. The vessel in front has two banks of oars. It carries a small poop covered by an awning for the commanding officer. It is steered by broad-bladed paddles on either quarter. The stern post curves over the top of the poop awning, and ends in an ornament composed of three curves, like feathers, and a gallery defended by an open latticed bulwark runs round the raised portion.

Two ranks of slaves pull the oars, the lower ranks within the upper. The upper row of oars are put through the latticed bulwark that protects a gallery running fore and aft the entire length of each side of the vessel. A man in the bow secures the rope by which she is moored.

This armed vessel has entered the port under the arch already referred to which stands apparently over the water joining the two ends of a mole, so as to span the entrance with some facility for closing it by means of a chain. The boats represented pass under it. It has one arch in the front, and the ends are pierced by smaller arches. It stands on a dado, has a shallow attic above the arch, on the top is a *quadriga*, a chariot drawn by four horses, intended probably to hold a statue of the conqueror. Outside the arch are other boats following the first one, and others rowing in the opposite direction carrying stores and ammunitions of war to a strong place represented in the next composition. Of those entering the arch one conveys four horses. It is a smaller boat than the first described, and is sculled by one rower. The stern of the boat rises high and turns over; it is square on the end, having bluff bows of the build still in use in Holland. One of the boats rowing away has two rowers and a steerer sitting in the stern, who manages a paddle on the boat's quarter. To this boat there is a flat deck or platform raised on four uprights high enough for the men to walk under. They appear to be soldiers, as two shields are on this platform overhead, and a soldier's knapsack and long-handled pot are hung to one of the uprights.

Inside the town in which these munitions are being stored the emperor is mustering and addressing the legions. The *signiferi* are round the spot on which he stands. Three standards of *manipuli* are to be distinguished. The emperor is without armour, and, besides his standard-bearer, is surrounded by a numerous guard.

An immediate advance is not made from this place, but the army appears about to be pushed across the river to a strong place, which is close to the theatre of the proposed campaign.

XXV.—*The emperor Trajan crosses the Tisia, Tibiscus (?) and prepares for action.*

Having collected sufficient material for his proposed operations, Trajan passes over or down the river, not by a bridge of boats as heretofore, but in various armed vessels, and this spot is probably at some distance from the Roman station last described. Two *liburnians* convey the emperor, his personal attendant, officers, and others to the fortified place from which he proposes to begin active operations. They are both rowed by two ranks of men and two banks of oars. The sides and stern have projecting gangways guarded by a bulwark of open rails and posts connected by crossed diagonal braces, as in the armed vessel first described. The vessel in the front conveys the emperor, who sits in the stern, protected by the covered awning already described. The bows of both vessels curve forward, like the breast of a swan, and are brought to an edge under water for the purpose of ramming in action. The sterns of the vessels curve gracefully forward, and the rope used for mooring or anchoring hangs round the cutwater, and is brought inboard round the bows. The vessel conveying Trajan has a carved panel on her bow, on which Telamon or Portumnus can be distinguished in a small sculptured bas-relief, with a steering paddle in hand, and a cupid on the tail of a marine monster behind. This minute piece of relief, indistinguishable from the distance of very few feet, is carefully and elegantly sculptured.

There are square panels or divisions in the raised bulwark at the bows of this vessel, holes or ports that could be opened at will with the purpose of annoying an enemy with missiles. These galleys in all their lines are gracefully designed and sit majestically on the water. The stern posts curve inwards and are ornamented as the first described. There is a steerer to the nearest vessel, and the steering paddle or rudder projects from the stern. In the further galley a man *rector* is armed with a stick wherewith to keep the oarsmen to their work. The landing of Trajan is accompanied by numerous boats bringing arms and munitions as well as by his officers and troops as in the last composition.

XXVI.—*Advance of the Roman legions.*

The emperor, with his two officers, addresses the troops and gives such instructions as are required. A body of cavalry is sent off at once to meet the enemy who employs that arm himself on this occasion. There are five horses sculptured. The riders are armed with shield and lance, and the lance of the foremost of them is represented in this instance. The whole four at the emperor's command are put in motion at the same time, and apparently the force is inferior to that of the enemy. Standard bearers in their bear skin head-pieces are fighting sword in hand and without their standard poles. German auxiliary troops armed with shields, supplied probably by the Romans, and with their own clubs, are in advance, going at the run. They wear breeches, but are otherwise nude.

The emperor himself, instead of giving directions from an eminence, is mounted and charges at the head of his men. He has a lance in his right hand, and holds his sheathed sword in his left. He has no covering to his head. Before him are two mounted soldiers giving information. They hold up their right hands, pointing over their shoulders in the direction in which the Romans are advancing. These are considered by Francke to be Prætorians.

In the foreground the Roman horses are accoutred with breast straps, to which are hung crescent ornaments of gilt bronze. There are the usual fringed saddle cloths; another has a bridle of rich chain work, and the heels of the riders are kicking the flanks of the horses. Opposed to them are the horsemen, allies of Decebalus. They are poorly mounted, but their horses or ponies seem to be active and well trained. Men and horses are covered with scale armour down to the feet and are without saddles. The enemy's cavalry is unable to sustain the shock of the Roman knights. One man is falling from his horse, another lies dead, others are in full flight. One rider turns and discharges an arrow at the pursuing Romans, but this part of the field is abandoned, and the scene is closed by a tree, of which the stem reaches the whole height of the spiral.

Another portion of this battle shows the Roman cavalry pursuing the Dacian infantry which has retired to their encampment. With the Roman cavalry are their infantry and auxiliary troops. The Germans are conspicuous in this action. Two of them in the foreground of the composition are urged on by a Roman legionary, who has a wounded Dacian before him. Another helps a Roman who engages two of the enemy. A Dacian in the background defends himself against two Germans. Various hand to hand combats occupy the rest of the field. A wounded Dacian raises his shield against the thrust of a *hasta* from a mounted Roman. Another, sitting in the foreground, tries to draw the broken point of a lance out of his breast.

The scene is laid in a rocky defile, which seems to have been occupied as a defensible post by the Dacians. Their camp equipage is seen on the level ground above. Three waggons are loaded, one with bags of corn, one with arms, shields, &c., and on the middle waggon are a Dacian dragon ensign, with various precious vessels. The waggons are four wheeled, and each has a pole and yoke so as to be drawn by two oxen. On the hind wheel of the left hand waggon a naked prisoner has been bound by the Dacians. He has been put to death by torture, and his limbs hang down over the wheel. Two dead bodies of Dacians are lying between the waggon and the combatants in the foreground. The battle has been fought by moonlight, and a graceful figure of a goddess Diana(?) is half seen over the rocks. She holds a scarf that forms an arch over her head. Her arms are nude, her breast covered by a mantle looped over each shoulder, and her head inclined as if looking over into the glen to watch the conflict and encourage her votaries, the Romans. A tree closes this portion of the conflict.

XXVII.—*Results of the action.*

The old men, women, and children fall into the hands of the Roman emperor. A man at the back of the composition has a child, clothed like the men, on his shoulder. His left hand holds the clasped hands of the child towards Trajan. A woman behind him stretches out her right hand to unite with them in this action. Another woman with a child at her breast turns to an old man who also carries a child on his shoulder holding on by the old man's hair. Another mother pushes her daughter before her, and two men in the foreground are supporting a little boy whose hands are held forward in supplication. Three men in the background seem to present this captive multitude to the emperor, to whom the officer on his right introduces them. The emperor is in the middle of an enclosure which is being fortified by a wall of masonry. Two soldiers make mortar in the foreground, one holding the basket in which it is contained. Others carry and lay hewn stones. Another is shaping a log of wood with a hammer and chisel. The emperor speaks to the captives and holds out his right hand as an assurance of protection.

XXVIII.—*The wounded and prisoners.*

Two wounded legionaries recline on the rock, and are tended by their comrades. Trajan is said to have torn his cloak into bandages on one occasion for the wounded, and this fact is perhaps meant to be represented here. One legionary is armed with a cuirass and shoulder plates. Two men support him; his helmet is off. Another, dressed in a linen frock or cuirass and neckerchief, has a wound in his thigh; a comrade in the same dress is binding it up. A prisoner on one knee, wearing the cap of a chief, has his arms bound behind his back by a Roman. Another is thrust forward by the hair. Another, wounded and seated on the ground with his hands bound behind him, turns his head, seeming to ask quarter of the soldier who holds him, and looks towards the emperor. In the background the legions are drawn up in order of battle. In the front are two *cornicenes*, with curved trumpets and four standards; two *dracones*, and two those of *manipuli*. On the tops of these last are small shields, eagles within wreaths under them, and mural ornaments. Behind the standards are drawn up the heavy troops in reserve. Two mules, each led by an armed soldier, are seen in the rear. They draw two *carrobalistæ*. The mules have bridle reins only, and are led, not driven. A chain is distinguishable round the neck of one, but there is no appearance of a yoke, and when in motion the engine was possibly lifted by a trail of some kind in the rear.

Fig. 42.

XXIX.—*General action.*

A battle in which the Roman army is engaged in all its force. The Roman cavalry is engaged all along the back ground of the composition hand to hand with Dacians on foot. The Romans have their shields hung or fixed to the pommels of their saddles, and fight with the lance. On one is a design of two large *anthemia* and a central boss. A Dacian shield in the middle line has a similar ornament with two stars. In the back line the Romans seem to have penetrated right through the Dacian ranks, but the latter have advanced close on the Roman reserves, and a body of them on the right of the composition fights desperately with both the light and heavy legionary troops, some of whom, as well as a German auxiliary, turn back to save this part of the field. The centre is held by Dacians fighting resolutely. Two Roman foot soldiers, one heavily armed, have penetrated the Dacian lines along with the cavalry. One of them, with his shield held under his left arm, holds the right hand of a Dacian, who is wounded and sitting on the ground, while with his left hand he grasps this man's beard, giving him quarter as to a prisoner. Dead and wounded Dacians are seen in the foreground. On the shield of one are four dolphins.

Behind the field of this conflict the emperor is standing. He holds a baton or roll, and is without arms. A soldier thrusts forward into his presence a Dacian whom he has taken prisoner and bound. On high ground above this scene are two *carrobalistæ*. Each carriage is in the form of a small single horse cart with two wheels. Three soldiers are engaged in discharging missiles from these engines. Two stoop down as if to bring the eye in position to take aim. The engines are not seen in profile, as their carriages are but fronting the spectator, so that the minor details of their construction cannot be distinctly made out. This is the first action during the war in which the Roman commander has recourse to artillery of this kind, and the numbers and valour of the enemy make it evident that the employment of these resources of military science is necessary. A tree closes the scene of the action.

XXX.—*Results of the fifth battle.*

The enemy is utterly discomfited, and the field of battle covered with his dead and wounded. In the background the survivors are in full flight. The emperor in his armour, with three officers unarmed, and wearing only the *pallium* or military cloak, is addressing his troops. He stands on a *suggestum*, or platform of turf or stones raised shoulder height for the occasion. His horses, three in number, each with plain bridles and fringed saddlecloths, are held beside him. Standard bearers hold three ensigns on one side. Two have busts, one a mural decoration, and two panels or drums, subdivided by crossed bands; all three have eagles amongst their decorations. Troops of all arms, including German auxiliaries, are present amongst the audience. To the left is a prætorian camp, enclosed by a temporary turf wall, over which are seen the heads of two guards and a multitude of prisoners. Two guards are before the entrance of the enclosure. A soldier carrying a sack of corn outside holds up his hand, and seems to applaud the speech and the generosity of the emperor. Two Romans belonging to the light troops embrace in the foreground, brothers or friends unexpectedly found alive by each other, probably Prætorians who are brought from different stations.

XXXI.—*The emperor distributing rewards to his soldiers.*

The emperor is seated on a folding seat and his two generals are beside him. A third officer unarmed appears to introduce the men selected for reward. One soldier bows and kisses the hand of the emperor. Five officers in the foreground in *pallia*, or cloaks, which are held up under each arm so as not to cover the figure below the middle, are watching and listening. The hands of two appear to express applause. The lifting of the hands is said by Francke to indicate that they are Prætorians. Their backs are turned to the spectator.

XXXII.—*Cruelty of the Dacians.*

Close to this dignified scene, from which it is not separated by any tree or sculptured detail, is shown a contrast in the behaviour of the enemy. Three Roman prisoners are stripped and brought out of a small gable roofed building, perhaps originally of Roman construction, to be tortured. Their arms are bound behind their backs, and five women are seen torturing them by applying lighted brands to their heads, arms, and shoulders. One woman drags down the head of a Roman by the hair, while another burns the back of his head, and a third the arm which is bound behind him. Another prisoner seems to implore compassion from a woman who puts the torch to his shoulder. The left leg is writhing under this infliction.

XXXIII.—*Trajan receives help from friendly natives.*

The emperor is surrounded by three officers. All, with one exception, wear the tunic and *pallium* clasped over the right shoulder; that of the emperor over the breast. One officer wears his cuirass. They are on the rocky bank of a river, outside the extreme angle of a fortified town, of which an arched gateway and a corner tower, with battlements, are behind the party. Two chiefs of friendly tribes or races are introduced to the emperor. Their hands are extended with a gesture implying confidence, and he stretches out his right hand to them. Two guards are present. These figures have no bonnet or head covering, There is an empty galley in the foreground, in which is a Roman officer or steward addressing the emperor, to whom this and other means of transport are being offered. The galley or row boat is similar to those used by the Romans. The curved stern post is turned back and ends in three bars or strips ; on the hip of the curved part is carved the head of a swan turned towards the stern. The covered cuddy or cabin appears to be tiled over with rounded shingles of oak or other wood carefully laid one over the other. On a panel outside the small forecastle in the bow of the vessel is a cupid riding on a hippocamp in the water, and small buttresses are carved on the upper edge. It is fronted by a projecting pointed nose or cutwater, and is intended as a guard boat. It carries seven oars besides the broad steering paddle. The former are worked through the open diagonal bulwark railing along the sides. With it is a boat with a raised poop, intended for transport purposes. She is laden with corn sacks and other stores closely packed and corded, which are being landed by the light troops. Amongst these stores are two standards. As standards would hardly have been sent to the legions as mere stores, it is probable that the *signiferi* have been sent with the soldiers in charge of the stores intended for special divisions or legions. A small building with a pedimental end can be distinguished behind these objects.

XXXIV.—*A river passage on a bridge of boats.*

The accumulation of warlike stores in a fortified place last described has been for the purpose of a further advance in force. Provisions and other munitions are represented as forming an unusually heavy baggage train, and the whole army is now advancing over a bridge of boats to take possession of a fortified place deserted by the enemy, and to penetrate a country difficult of access and of uncertain resources.

The boats in this bridge are four in number only. They are of different build from those shown in the construction of the bridge thrown over the Danube, being smaller and without the raised poop seen in the former case. The sterns are of the same form raised and cut square at the top, the bows ending in a point. They are such boats as are still in use on many rivers in Italy. The bridge has a boarded fence or bulwark on which is a latticed railing. Piles are not driven into the bed of the river to steady the end of the platform. Three led horses, with shields fastened between the saddle and the saddlecloth, precede the emperor, the bridle of each is held by a soldier dressed in the linen cuirass, but without arms or head piece. An attendant soldier armed in a similar cuirass and neckerchief follows these, and immediately in front of the emperor, who is without the superior officers usually seen with him. His left hand holds the pommel of his sheathed sword, and the right holds up his mantle. He is followed close by the *signiferi* who bear five standards. Three are those of the *manipuli*. Of the other two, one is an *aquila,* and the other is surmounted by a *ram* standing on an oblong bracket into which the top of the shaft of the ensign is fixed.

This particular ensign appears here for the first and last time. It is here displayed as a sign that the legion will take part in siege operations.

Behind the *signiferi* march the legionaries whom an officer turns and addresses, apparently ordering them to begin the march. They issue from an arched gateway abutting immediately on the river and from which the platform of the bridge begins. The wall above it is battlemented. At some distance behind, a battlemented wall can be distinguished which is pierced by two arched windows.

XXXV.—*Occupation of a fort.*

Immediately on landing on the further bank a portion of Trajan's forces occupy a fortified place belonging to and deserted by the enemy. It has a wall of masonry at the front. A frame raised on two lofty posts on the front of the wall shows the remains of one of the machines or *balistœ* used by the enemy, and the wall ends in a round tower of masonry, the wall of which is continued round the inner side. Two lofty posts or poles appear to have been portions of another warlike engine, but the top part is concealed by one of the stair windows of the column. The other sides of the place, or of this part of it, are defended by palisades of timber pointed at the top and set close together. Beyond this are seen two carts, one drawn by horses and carrying shields, spears, and sacks of corn; the other drawn by bullocks, laden with arms and sacks, a horse saddled and bridled, and a sumpter horse with a large package on his back.

XXXVI.—*Trajan addressing his troops.*

Beyond the first part of the fortifications of this place the ground rises to an *arx* or citadel on a rocky platform. It is ascended by a stair and the side of the cliff is protected by a close fence of planks nailed to latticed rails. A similar wooden structure leads to a higher portion of the fort. In this side of it are two gate posts and wooden constructions are seen over the wall. A zigzag wall shown in plan runs from this upper *arx* down the edge of a precipitous cliff to the foreground. In the angles each side of this wall or bank are small diamond-shaped enclosures, and at intervals close to the edges of the wall inside and out spots intended to represent wall engines. These fortifications are all shown by the artist in plan. An arched doorway at the bottom of the rock outside the wall appears to be intended as a sally port and to communicate with some subterraneous entrance. On the flat rocky eminence the emperor surrounded by his two general officers addresses his legionaries. One of the officers turns to him and seems to enumerate or introduce to the emperor the heads of the column.

XXXVII.—*Reception of a Dacian ambassador.*

Trajan is surrounded by *signiferi*, one carries an *aquila* another a *draco* and a strong guard. Two men, one dressed in a linen tunic tied in at the waste, notched at the bottom, with another under dress reaching half way down the thigh, short cloak fastened on the right shoulder, drawers to the calf of the leg, and sandals ; the other, in a similar dress behind, addresses the emperor. The principal personage appears to invite the emperor to treat of peace. The latter stretches out his right hand as if stating conditions. A square *arx* is behind them. Inside the walls are two square look-out places raised on posts of timber above the heights of the walls protected by a balustrade of upright and diagonal crossed rails. A square gate, with a portcullis, is seen in the front wall, and one of the wooden towers is immediately over it. A roofed building and two small houses are seen inside.

XXXVIII.—*Reception of another ambassador.*

Trajan attended by his two lieutenants receives two men on embassy. They are cloaked and dressed in the usual Dacian trowsers (not as the personage last received by the emperor.) They appear by the action of the hands to remonstrate against the severity of conditions offered them. The emperor holds his cloak in the left hand, and seems by the action of the right to insist on his terms. Meanwhile a walled enclosure is being prepared.

XXXIX.—*Sacrifice of the suovetaurilia.*

A fortified camp semicircular in form with a prætorian gate in one flank and another wider in the right wall. These walls are battlemented, and two tents, one a hut with arched entrance perhaps to be left permanently, both are roofed with planks. Inside a sacrifice is being offered by the emperor dressed. In this way the new campaign opens as did the last.

XL.—*The Emperor addresses the Troops.*

Trajan stands on a bank, not on a *suggestum*, made for the purpose. He is attended as usual, grasps his sheathed sword below the hilt with his left hand, and suits the action of the right to the matter of his address. Three *signiferi*, with two standards on the bank, and a crowd of common soldiers in the foreground appear to listen with great attention.

XLI.—*Laying of a Road.*

The country is densely wooded. Soldiers are employed cutting the trees which are carefully laid together to form a road, such as are still known as "corduroy" roads in Canada. Longitudinal sleepers are laid over and under these, and broken stones and concrete above the timber. The road lies along the Danube.

A woodcut represents this construction, Fig. 28 in the preface, p. 70.

Two small buildings covered with a roof of planks nailed to the wall plates and ridge beams below them are distinguishable in the forest. Two heads of spies or prisoners are stuck on spears beside one of the buildings, perhaps those of assassins mentioned in the introduction, p. 83.

XLII.—*Fortifications of the Enemy destroyed.*

The emperor on horseback, followed by two mounted attendants, crosses a stream by a bridge of timber erected by the enemy. It is defended by a wooden enclosure of timber palisading. A gateway is defended by a roofed wooden structure erected over it. This enclosure or gate house has four windows. All these wooden defences are set on fire by the Romans.

Three men form a guard to defend the hither end of the bridge. It is raised on piles driven into the bed of the river. A central opening seems to be left by a wider disposition of the piles, so that the navigation of the stream might not be hindered. The parapet is a stout upright railing with the usual diagonal bracing between. All the timber is carefully squared, and the piles are ornamented with capitals. A close piece of paling forms the parapet over the central part of the bridge, and on the further bank a structure of close paling seems to indicate a continuation of the bridge over soft ground.

In the distance are seen a body of Dacians with a standard, pointing to the emperor whom they see without being discovered, and prudently beating a retreat.

XLIII.—*Construction of a fortified camp.*

On the rocky ground close to the bridge, the emperor is constructing a fortified camp. Part of it is of masonry and is square, though represented in false perspective by the sculptor. Great activity is shown in pushing on the completion of this stronghold.

This square fort is distinct from the rest of the fortified camp, which is defended by a high *agger*, perhaps of turf, with occasional battlements. Inside is a small tower with a chamber in it which has a window higher than the wall of circumvallation. Two huts roofed with planks are also to be distinguished. The place is surrounded by rocks on which are a few trees.

XLIV.—*Submission of a Dacian chief.*

Outside the prætorian gate of his camp stands the emperor, behind him are the two guards. One of his officers is beside him, the other presents to him a Dacian chief or prince. He wears the usual dress and a cap on his head ; he is kneeling, throws his shield on the ground at the feet of Trajan and implores mercy. The emperor with his left hand on his sword hilt makes the Dacian a sign to rise with his right. Two *cornicines*, an eagle, two signiferi of manipuli, and a column of soldiers complete the ceremonial of this reception.

XLV.—*Advance of a provision train.*

Two carts drawn by horses are following the army, which is supposed to have advanced to a fresh post. The carts have two wheels, of six spokes, and are balanced over the axletrees. Each contains two large casks, hooped in the centre and at each end. The casks are supported by blocks of wood to prevent motion in the carts. The provision train is guarded by soldiers.

XLVI.—*A fortified camp.*

On a piece of rocky and broken ground a fortified camp
has been placed. Two tents are seen inside. Three guards
are standing sentry outside the Pretorian gate. In the distance, partly hidden in the hollows and depressions of the
ground, are four small round temples, each is fronted by a
doorway with ornamental jambs, and moulded lintel over it.
One of these doors is topped by a circular pediment. Another
door is arched, and has two side columns with a corona
above them, making an outer door frame. Each building
has a conical roof, and in the roofs of three are dormer
windows covered in with flat tiles or planks sloping back to
the roof. Two cypress trees are seen beside each of these
buildings, and these buildings are perhaps tombs or mortuary
temples. They are scattered amongst broken rocks which
half conceal the Roman soldiers, whom the sculptor has
represented amongst them. Further off is another detached
fortified enclosure. It has a wall of masonry, in which is
a square headed door, and besides that a prætorian gate or
opening in the wall defended by two wooden towers.

XLVII.—*Trajan advances his troops.*

The emperor, attended by his two lieutenants, is standing
on a bank or shelf of rock. Three guards, with oval shields,
wearing the linen cuirass, are in attendance. Behind are
the *signiferi* and the columns of legionaries. In advance of
the emperor is a body of Mauritanian cavalry. The riders
are without covering on the head or feet and wear only a
long mantle wrapper, part of which forms a skirt, the ends
are clasped over the shoulders by brooches, and hang loose
before and behind, leaving the arms free. Their horses
have neither saddles nor bridles distinguishable, but a double
rope passes round the necks over the shoulders, perhaps to
use in tethering. They have long tails and flowing manes.
The men have large round shields, no arms are represented
in the sculpture, but the action of the hands shows that
they all carry a lance. One man, an officer, holds up his
right hand to encourage his men.

XLVIII.—*Defeat and flight of the enemy.*

The enemy is seen broken and defeated at the edge of
this rocky defile. Two resolute men make head against

the cavalry. The corner of this composition is filled with dead and wounded men.

The Dacians retreat into the forest. A dragon ensign is carried away by the band.

XLIX.—*A further advance and fresh fortifications.*

In this composition, while the light troops of Trajan are again sent forward, a new fortification is begun. This is a rocky height naturally strong. It is square in outline, with the corners of the enclosure rounded off. The four conventional gates are made, and lofty timber gate posts are dropped into the stone sockets made to receive them by workmen belonging to the legions. Within the enclosure are several inequalities amongst the rock in which parties of workmen carrying hewn stones to form battlements are nearly hidden. In a deep fosse or ditch round the outer circuit of the walls other workmen are giving orders and industriously digging out sand and gravel to form mortar. In the circuit of the prætorian camp, inside of which there is a tent, a doorway with two closed valves is seen, and above it is a strong framework of wood. Close beside it, mounted on the summit of the wall, is placed a *balista*, and another is mounted on another side of the enclosure. All these means of protection indicate a country favourable for ambush and surprise, and they are precautions not hitherto taken in the fortification of Roman stations in Dacia.

L.—*Trajan receives two Native Chiefs.*

Trajan attended as usual receives two chiefs, to whom he gives his right hand in token of protection. They are on ground lower than that on which the emperor is standing, and their feet are not seen. The advance of the army is continued.

LI.—*A Battle in the Forest.*

On the right of the composition is a large space enclosed within a rampart of logs. The timbers are laid longways and across with the greatest regularity.

The artist has tried to represent some parts of this accumulation of timber in perspective. Two soldiers in the foreground within the enclosure are busy manœuvering a *balista,* seen in the accompany- ing woodcut, while a third removes a piece of timber for the works in progress in the rear, which a fourth begins to shape with his axe. Within and about this pile of wood are the mailed ranks of the legions, drawn up as rallying lines for the *velites* and auxiliary forces sent on to attack in the front.

Fig. 43.

There the battle is maintained with determination on both sides. On that of the Romans there are German auxiliaries, nude to the waist, and armed with clubs and shields, with which they engage the better armed Dacians. Besides the Germans are archers in peaked helmets and coats of mail, and a number of slingers, the latter wear loose tunics tied at the waist and *saga,* cloaks, in the folds of which, with left arm, they hold a number of stones, which are cast from a sling made of a thong of leather and two cords. They wear a shield on the left arm. The enemy fights with tenacity, and dead and wounded of both armies are lying at the feet of the combatants. The Roman soldiers engaged in this action are seen throwing the *hasta,* or striking with that weapon held by the middle of the haft. The field of battle is amongst the trees of the forest. To the extreme right, in rear of the combatants, a soldier is hurrying a *carrobalista* to the front. The machine itself is not seen in profile, but it does not differ from those sculptured elsewhere on the column. The enemy is seen feeding the battle with fresh troops, who hurry through the forest to meet the Romans. Of the latter one is seen in the heart of the Dacian host.

The enemy is busy in his rear cutting down trees to fortify a strong position taken up on the high ground above the scene of the combat. On this the enemy has mounted on his fortifications a *balista* such as are used by the Romans. The enclosure is of timber and stones, as explained in page 54 of the introduction, strongly braced together, and seems to be intended as a refuge for their beaten forces, as they are seen in various defiles among the rocks hurry- ing in the direction of this fortified camp. A dragon and a standard in the form of the Roman *draco* or *labarum* are carried forward in the same direction. Several men, both in these ranks and in those in the foreground, are covered with the Dacian cap indicating their rank. Two stone towers in the rear of the Dacian battle are of uncertain attribution. One is placed at the end of a tongue or promontory of high ground. It is built on the edge of a cliff, and strong walls of pointed timber palisades defend the only accessible sides of the tower, the doors of which appears to be approached from the high ground by a drawbridge, so as to be wholly secure from attack. This tower is without a roof, and the hollow top is shewn in perspective. There are fugitives wandering round the defiles between these towers, and two Dacians are cutting timber in the foreground. This whole composition is cut off from the next by the trunk of a tree.

LII.— *A Roman fortification and examination of a prisoner.*

The Romans advance beyond the position of the enemy, who is now pressed and are busily employed fortifying a stronghold, so as to make good the ground now acquired. An unusually strong guard is placed to protect the legionaries employed in these operations. The two principal figures amongst the guards are two of the Prætorians, and these figures are amongst the most dignified and best designed in the whole series.

In the background, while superintending these fortifications, the emperor receives and examines a prisoner. He is bound and thrust into the presence of Trajan by his captors. The emperor is attended by his two general officers and by his guard. These constructions and fortifications are no hindrance to the progress of the Roman arms, and the men are seen advancing.

LIII.—*Attack and defeat of the enemy.*

Trajan again attacks the enemy. The van of the Roman army is composed of auxiliaries of the same nationalities as those employed in the last great battle. The Germans are nude to the waist, and have no offensive weapons but clubs ; a figure in a loose tunic in the foreground holds a number of stones in a fold of his coat with his left arm. He is not slinging, but throwing these with his right. Archers in jerkins or short frocks of scaled mail and conical head-pieces are beyond these barbarous skirmishers, and beyond them come the lighter troops of the legion, behind whom are drawn up the *gravis armatura* in rallying lines and columns. The enemy is pressed back to his fortifications; numbers lie dead, but the fight is maintained stoutly nevertheless. The shields of the Romans and Dacians in rival lines are seen crashing together in the shock of battle. A Dacian is kneeling that he may thrust his own shield within the guard of that of his adversary so as to deliver a fair blow with his weapon.

The enemy cannot long stand the Roman charge, and is seen pressed back into a stronghold fortified with palisades and planks, in which he seeks refuge, leaving the ground strewed with his dead and wounded. Part of this fort is covered in, and part an open court fortified in the manner already described.

A desperate stand appears to have been made on all sides of this fort or enclosure. The enemy defends himself from within it, and the Romans advance and storm the place by means of the peculiar formation for attack known as the *testudo.* They hold their shields, which are oblong, square, and curved, so as to lap slightly over each other over their heads and backs, and a similar use of the shield defends the flank of the column of attack. Of them, accordingly, in this bas-relief we see the legs only. The slope of the whole surface of shields protects the men so well that ordinary missiles, even stones of great weight rolled down the slope harmlessly, the shock of impact being in the case of stones, &c. distributed over so large a surface. The walls do not seem to require a second rank over the first, or if so the artist has not shown it. The legs of the men supporting the *testudo* are in exact and studied regularity of posture, so as to give full effect to their power of support when thus combined.

The enemy tries with sword and shield to make some impression on the attack, but in vain, and the place is carried by storm.

LIV.—*The emperor receives assurances of victory.*

The emperor, according to Dion Cassius, ascended the mountains, and followed Decebalus into his last retreat; and we see him in this composition standing on a rock, with his two general officers and surrounded by soldiers, giving accounts of the result of the last actions, and of another next to be described. The whole composition is well disposed, the emperor standing between two groups of men. Rocks are seen rising to the top of the spiral behind him, and forest and broken ground in front. Two soldiers hold up heads of men they have killed, in order to claim the imperial favour.

LV.—*Last battle of the war.*

Trajan presses forward to the stronghold of Decebalus. The light troops and auxiliaries are in advance, and the heavy troops are drawn up in the rear. A man in a linen tunic and cloak is hurling stones, and a German, nude to the waist, fighting with a club, but it is not rendered in the sculpture.

The Roman troops most in advance are desperately engaged and fight hand-to-hand with the sword. Two of them are engaging a wounded Dacian, borne to the ground, and without his shield, but fighting with desperation, as is shown in the determined expression of his eyes and mouth. Another Roman climbs over heaps of slain to reach those still resisting. A stockaded fort is seen in the background, and ranks of Dacians are half distinguished in a defile of the rocks which separate them from the Roman attack. They express uncertainty and dismay by the action of their hands. Some are rushing on determined to dispute the ground still, and others seem inclined to take refuge in the fort, which is a timber structure with heavy timber posts at intervals, and a gate fixed into equally heavy pieces of timber.

LVI.—*The Dacians are totally defeated.*

The emperor constructs fortifications, and holds a council of war. The emperor, attended as usual by Lucius Quietus and the tribunes of the legions, is seen raised on a *suggestum* inside a square fortified building of masonry. It is battlemented, and an arched doorway is found in the corner shown in the bas-relief. The door jambs are Doric pilasters, and the arch is moulded; men are employed hewing and squaring timber to complete these defensive works. The officers immediately round Trajan wear feathered plumes in their helmets. The emperor is stretching out his right hand, and appears to give emphasis by this action to various propositions or conditions which he is laying down, and to the principles on which he intends to guide his conduct in regard to the rebellion of Decebalus and his treatment of the conquered people, so as to secure the tranquility of these outlying provinces for the future.

Stores of timber are in course of accumulation on the ground now to be built over.

LVII.—*Construction of other and larger fortifications.*

The emperor establishes another and a more commodious military station well placed, and where water is abundant. At the right-hand side of the composition, and under the protection of a large round tower, part of a permanent enclosure, is seen a fountain issuing in a plentiful stream from the rock, from which it is received in a long basin of masonry of irregular shape. A soldier without his helmet, but bearing his oval shield on his left arm, is dipping a vessel into the basin. Another soldier drinks, and another carries away with him a vessel, with a handle, full of water to his quarters. Two other men are carrying closely packed sacks of grain into the fortress. Two armed attendants wearing military cloaks hold two horses of the emperor in the foreground. Is this Ulpia Trajana?

Another part of the fortifications is shown of irregular shape with a gate closed by a door in two valves in one angle. Over the gate is a *cataracta* or wooden portcullis. Into this part soldiers are seen carrying grain.

LVIII.—*Trajan receives Decebalus and determines the conditions of peace.*

The emperor is seated on a chair or throne tastefully draped, and elevated on a *suggestum* about three feet high. He is attended by several officers of high rank. Five of these personages are dressed in cuirasses. In rear of the persons thus dressed in the foreground is a guard of three soldiers. On the other side are the *signiferi*, of whom six are represented bearing the standards of various *manipuli*. Outside all is a strong guard of Prætorians.

In the foreground immediately below the emperor is the Dacian King Decebalus on his knees, with his hands raised to the knees of Trajan imploring forgiveness and peace. Two other chiefs are kneeling on one knee immediately in front of him. All three wear the Dacian cap. The shields and swords of the last two are laid beside them. Five men stand bound behind them, they are prisoners of importance reserved to grace the imperial triumph in Rome.

Behind these prisoners a crowd of Dacian chiefs, some wearing the cap, kneel and stretch out both hands imploring the clemency of Trajan. Behind stand the rest of the Dacian officers using the same action of the hands. Their shields are laid down on the ground. Two dragon ensigns and two *labara* short flags on a cross bar like the Roman

dracones, are held behind, and are supposed to be sur-
rendered like the arms. This is one of the conditions
imposed by Trajan.

Fig. 44.

As in the last composition we distinguish various wooden
cataractæ, and other details of fortification on the walls;
stretching behind the entire scene is a range of fortifications, some of logs, some of timber and stone, as described in
page 54 of the introduction; they are given in the accompanying woodcut; and fortifications of sawn timber are
represented adjoining the parts of wall still in progress.

LIX.—*Fulfilment of further conditions of the peace.*

Dacians are seen destroying with axes and hammers the
stone and other fortifications. Battlemented walls, gates,
small temples, and other buildings, with pedimental roofs,
and framed doors are distinguishable amongst the con-
demned works. They represent Zarmizegethusa, the principal
stronghold of Decebalus in this part of his dominions, and

show how much the enemy had borrowed of the architecture and other arts of the Romans, and give some indication of the advancement made in these respects by Decebalus under former Roman emperors.

Return of the Inhabitants expelled by Decebalus.

One of the conditions to be carried into execution by the Dacians was the surrender of lands and settlements, from which they had ejected the former inhabitants, to the original owners. Accordingly women carrying children at the breast; old men with children on their shoulders; a mother with an infant tied up and in a wooden cradle on her head, are returning either to quarters evacuated by the Dacians, or, as seems more in accordance with their dress and appearance, they are the unarmed Dacian population returning with their cattle.

LX.—*Trajan gives his parting instructions before leaving for Rome.*

The thirteenth legion to which was given the title of Dacica, had been stationed hitherto in Upper Pannonia. It was now to be entrusted with the safe keeping of the conquered country, from which the emperor was about to start in order to celebrate his triumph in Rome. The place in which the last stronghold has been taken and the fortifications of Ulpia Trajana commanded by Trajan have been constructed is north of the Banat, somewhere on the confines of Hungary and Transylvania, and from the rocky nature of the ground represented, probably on one of the spurs that start northward from the southern Carpathian chain.

The emperor and·his two generals are on a high *suggestum* of stone finished with a moulding or projecting edge. He and they are unarmed. He wears a loose tunic, over which is the *chlamys* or military cloak, not the· civil *toga*, and boots tied over the instep. In his left hand he holds what is perhaps a scroll or written commission or record of his wishes. Before him are the *signiferi* with three upright standards and an eagle. Three of the soldiers present are bearers of these ensigns; ten more are probably tribunes. All are dressed in their linen cuirasses and military cloaks; they are without helmets and unarmed.

The emperor is giving detailed instructions, and with the forefinger of his right hand seems to dwell on each separate head of the instructions he leaves behind him. The two general officers are apparently numbering off each point with the forefinger. The tribunes hold out each his right hand in token of pledging his faith to keep the oath exacted by the Emperor.

Thus ends the first Dacian War.

LXI.—*Figure of Victory and trophies erected in honour of the war.*

In the middle, between two trophies, a graceful figure of Victory is represented writing the words *Vic. Dac.* on a shield. She is winged, one wing is folded upright, the other reaches out horizontally as if she had just alighted on the spot. She is draped in a long *peplum*, with loose sleeves ; the right sleeve is looped at the shoulder, but has slipped off half way down to the elbow exposing her graceful neck and shoulder. Her mantle is thrown over the left shoulder and brought round in front, where the two ends are twisted one into the other, from the hips it falls in graceful folds to the ground. Her hair is drawn off the forehead and knotted at the back of the head. Her left foot is raised on a Sarmatian or Dacian helmet, which is laid at the base of a small square altar.

Her left arm is thrown over the upper edge of an oval shield that rests on the altar, and she holds a *stilus* in her right hand with which she is about to commemorate the Dacian conquests. The shield is plain with a narrow rim of laurel leaves round it. It will be observed that this figure is little altered from the traditional type and attitude of the Victory of the Athenian temple of wingless Victory, though her foot is raised in that bas-relief, in order to untie her sandal. In the case of the Venus de Milo (a Victory ?) now in the Louvre, the action of the hands and the feet have been identical with this composition.

On the right and left of the victory are two trophies, that to the right (spectator's left) is composed of a Dacian cloak on a tree. On the summit is a conical helmet, with cheek pieces ornamented with vertical bands and quatrefoils. On the arms or transverse beam are hung shields. Dacian *dracones* and spears are crossed behind these shields. On the ground below are eight shields, one with a wreath in the centre. A helmet on the ground, another resting on the central shield, two *dracones*, a crooked scimetar, two *lubara* cut into three deep notches at the bottom, a sheaf of arrows, and a short spear complete this trophy.

The centre of the left hand trophy is a scale cuirass over a loose tunic, and with a *sagum* draped round the neck and shoulders. Right and left are crossed shields, two spears and a sword one side, two spears the other, arranged between the pairs of shields, two *dracones*. A long straight sword with richly ornamented scabbard hangs by a shoulder belt over the coat of mail on the right side. Below are six shields, two helmets, a *labarum*, two *dracones*, two broad bladed hammer-backed axes, three spears, two helmets, a crooked scimetar, and a round empty quiver, perhaps a straight trumpet complete the arms in this trophy. Models of small architectural elevations, such as temples, &c. are added in the background of this left-hand trophy.

End of the first Dacian war.

LXII.—*Second Dacian war, A.D.* 104.

This first bas-relief represents the departure of the emperor with his officers and troops in a convoy of armed vessels from the Roman head-quarters on the Save. In the extreme right of the composition is a palace. It is an oblong building, roofed, and with a peristile in *antis* of engaged columns round the walls. The columns are at irregular distances giving room for windows, closed, with gratings between. On the end façade between two pairs of columns is a square recess containing a statue of a female deity. The central building is surrounded by a colonnade roofed over and closed on the outer side by a wall, in which are windows. Another building with four columns in the front, a long roofed building without windows are also seen, and a number of arched porches surround the port. In the foreground is a mole, on the end of which is a triumphal arch. It has one arch only, and on the top are erected three statues. The centre figure has one foot raised on a pedestal, and holds a club in his left hand, Hercules or Mars. The two standing figures right and left hold up each the arm that is nearest the central figure. This arch also has something of the character of those erected by Trajan at Ancona and Beneventum.

The emperor is standing in the stern of an armed vessel rowed by two ranks of rowers. There are gangways along her sides, and a similar passage carried on wooden brackets round the stern. There is an arched cabin aft, carefully covered in with planks, which are kept in place by narrow external ribs. A large piece of timber, cut into broad flat labels on the inner end, curves forward from the top of her stern post over the cabin, while a carved piece curves back over the stern post like the neck of a swan. From the carved end hangs a lantern which is round, with conical cover, and a straight bar fastened to the sides for a handle. From the centre of this it is hung. Men on the quay are holding out flaming torches showing us that the lantern is hung there to indicate which is the imperial vessel, and that it is night. The emperor is in civil dress. He is standing and his left hand shows by its action that he is giving his orders to the commanders of the vessels forming the convoy.

A *draco* standard is hoisted in the emperor's galley. The cutwater of the galley projects on the level of the water. Her bow is built up inside into a forecastle, the outside of which is panelled in horizontal divisions, in which are carvings. Three small panels contain dolphins and architectural ornaments in relief, and hippocamps are also carved on a larger scale in relief on the bows at her water line.

A galley behind that of Trajan has bands of carved ornament round the bows, and a series of arches round her forecastle. Part of a foremast is shown in this galley, and a lateen sail reefed up to a yard, which swings across the front of the mast. Two ends of rope for hoisting the sail aloft are coiled round the end of mast shown. Another, nearest the spectator, has a carved forecastle front. The cutwater projects like the snout of a swordfish, and an eye is carved upon it. The commander stands to listen to the emperor, and the action of his left hand seems to command his oarsmen to stop, or row easy while the orders of Trajan are given. In the stern of this galley, which is without the curved stern timber, are three standards, with wreaths, wreathed busts, and small shields surmounting the tops. Besides these a *draco* is hoisted over the stern, the pole appearing just above the stern post of the vessel. Ahead of these liburnian galleys are seen the noses of dolphins and other fish among the waters.

LXIII.—*Reception of the emperor.*

The Roman fleet makes for one of the more important colonies founded by the emperor on the Danube. A port surrounded by quays built on arches shows that a ship basin has been dug out, or a mole built into the water. For this the vessels are all making. There is open space for landing and embarking between the buildings of the town and the edge of the water. On a point of land beyond the quays is seen an altar on which fire is burning, and before it a dead bull, showing that a sacrifice to Neptune[33] has been offered for the safe arrival of the emperor. The open space or esplanade is surrounded by colonnades, supporting a flat architrave, from which springs a roof. The inner side is walled, but it is open to the port, and this is provided for stowage of merchandise and stores. Behind a large square building can be distinguished a crowd of eager citizens with women and children, who are hurrying to the water's edge to welcome the emperor. The men wear the Roman *toga*. The women are dressed as Roman matrons, and a child in front of them is in loose drapery. The emperor is on shore and is received with enthusiasm by the colonists. The quay on which he stands communicates by steps or a sloping road with the rest of the town, and is defended at this point by a lofty round tower in several stories, opening on the two upper stories with windows, which command a view on every side. A wide arched opening on the tower of these stories seems intended for a *pharos* or lighthouse.

The emperor is surrounded by a crowd of military colonists wearing the tunic and *sagum*, or military cloak, who hasten on in advance to bring him into their city. Others of higher rank, wearing the *toga*, seem to have landed from two galleys moored under the tower. The foremost holds a scroll in his left hand. All lift their right hands in token of respect and welcome. Three men in the galley, furthest from the spectator, are in the act of landing, and are observing the scene from the decks. Sailors in the foremost galley are making her secure. The bows of their galley, besides the protruding cutwater, are armed with two bars of iron projecting forwards from under her forecastle, the upper ending in a ram's head of bronze. An *insigne* or flag on a pole with flower ornament on the top has been struck and laid flat.

LXIV.—*Triumphal procession.*

The whole city seems to have accompanied the emperor, and a number of men are crowned with garlands. Their wives and a number of children accompany the procession. They are preceded by a number of the legionaries in civil dress, amongst whom are two *lictors* bearing *fasces*.

---

[33] See Introduction, p. 61.

A number of bearded men, colonists, are amongst this crowd. All seem to wear shoes, and the children are draped, the boys in the toga, and the girls in long *peplæ* and veils, which are draped over the shoulder and fall in graceful folds down to their feet. One little girl holds the hand of a boy, and with the other hand expresses wonder and delight. The Roman officers and attendants, and the crowned procession in their rear, pass under a triumphal arch.

LXV.—*The emperor about to offer a sacrifice.*

Two altars are seen. One is ornamented with lines of moulding on the upper edge and a plinth below. The other is of stones laid together, and is temporary. Garlands are hung on the four sides of each altar. Fire burns on each. The emperor is at the temporary altar, and appears to be commanding silence by the action of his right hand. Two bulls are held behind the two altars, and two others are in the foreground. Behind is a fortified *prætorium*, entered by a door covered with close horizontal planking, and defended by a *cataracta*. Two soldiers fully armed are mounting guard within.

LXVI.—*Another landing and sacrifice.*

The emperor is collecting the forces placed in various garrisons. He is here at another colonial city at the port of which he has landed. In the background is a range of buildings, the most important being a theatre. The front is to the spectator. Rows of windows or open arched corridors are seen round the exterior of the circular part, and the rows of seats are shown in perspective over the top. A lofty archway joins this building to an open colonnade. Cypresses and other trees are seen in a garden beyond. The walls of the town and a raised arched gateway are seen to the right. To the left of the theatre is a building in two stories, the lower entered by a lofty arch, then a temple with a portico on four Ionic columns and other buildings. In front of these buildings is a wide quay supported by arches rising from the water. On the right a galley touches the quay, and legionaries and three standard bearers are partly on the shore, and others in the act of landing.

An awning is spread over the seats of the galley on a spar, of which one end rests on the top of the forecastle. Hippocamps and a cupid are carved on the bow and an eye behind her beak. The sterns of other vessels are discernible over the walls at another quay or landing place.

The emperor is in the act of offering sacrifice on a small square altar. Firebrands are upon the altar, and a pine cone, pomegranates, and other fruit are prepared for consumption. Besides ministers there are citizens or soldiers and their children, both boys and girls. The crowd covers the entire space of the quay or platform of the port.

LXVII.—*Trajan departs with fresh forces for the war.*

The scene is a seaport at which fresh troops probably belonging to another legion have disembarked. A large sailing transport is at anchor inside the harbour. She has open railed bulwarks, and a gallery similarly protected is carried on brackets over her stern. This gallery projects over the stern post, which is carried up and curved gracefully over backwards, and carved in the shape of a swan's neck. A tall mast amidships is stayed down by three ropes or shrouds to the sides of the ship. A yard to which a square sail is closely reefed is hoisted on this mast, and ropes from either end of the yard are carried forward to keep the sail from swinging out of its place. An anchor is cast over the side. The shank of the anchor is of great length. The stock is of iron like the rest, and there is a ring on the upper end of the shank as well as another at the junction of the flukes so as to secure it at sea. A hemp cable is looped over the anchor. The usual paddle or rudder swings over her quarter, where it is secured by a broad loop of metal. The handle is hooked at the top. On a hill above the port is a building covered with planks.

A number of legionaries have disembarked from the vessel just described and are following.

A horse richly caparisoned, but without saddle, is loaded with shields, and is led along with the standards. A building roofed over, and with a square window on the upper story, is distinguished behind this part of the line.

LXVIII.—*The column reaches another colony.*

In front of the legionaries march a body of men, officers perhaps, who hold lances, but have no shields or cuirasses. Immediately in front of these persons are the cavalry. They have saddles of rich stuff and clothes under, and the

shields are carried flat against the flank of the horse under
the saddlecloths, and are kept in place by the legs of the
riders.[34]

Buildings in the background indicate the approach to a
colony with a town and fortifications.

LXIX.—*The emperor welcomed by colonists.*

The emperor is on horseback at the head of the line
of march. He is unarmed and in civic dress. His horse
is more plainly caparisoned than those of his officers.
He is met on the outside of a large archway of masonry
by a number of natives of neighbouring tribes or Dacians
who are under Roman rule. They wear the loose trousers,
ample gowns, and mantle of the Dacians, all wear shoes.
There are no women amongst them, but several children,
one is a girl. The dress of the boys is in every respect
that of Dacians in miniature. The girl wears a loose gown
reaching to the feet, and a loose shawl reaching to the
middle tied round the waist. All the men and children
stretch their hands to the emperor imploring his protection.

LXX.—*The emperor offers sacrifice.*

Immediately inside the arched entrance to the place an
altar is dressed and hung with garlands. Several children
are round the altar. Behind are native colonists with their
wives and children coming to do honour to the sacrifice.
One woman holds a child in her arms, whose attitude has
suggested some of the compositions of the Madonna of
Raphael, a veil over her head confines the hair, and falls
gracefully down the back of the neck. She wears a long
peplum, and an upper robe is knotted gracefully in front
below her waist. The back of another shows this loose
robe knotted also between the shoulder blades, to prevent
it from falling over the arms, and it is gathered at the
waist.

LXXI.—*Fresh fortifications.*

A number of colonists, Roman and native, are employed
felling trees. One man holding an adze is giving direc-

---

[34] The Nubian hunters of the Upper Nile described by Sir Samuel Baker,
who attack the elephant with the sword only, carry their weapons, which are
of excessive sharpness, between the thigh and the horse in this fashion.

tions. Several lengths of railings or framework to be placed on the crest of walls are in preparation. These are differently put together, some are framed with upright posts and single diagonal braces from the head of one to the foot of the others. Others are latticed girders, such as we make at the present day. The men are not in armour of any kind, nor are helmets or weapons to be seen. They are not, therefore in the presence of the enemy, not as yet at the actual scene of hostilities.

Besides the carpenters, masons are employed, and a basket of lime and concrete is seen emptied on a wall. There are two enclosures in process of construction. The nearest has within it a small house of two stories, with a round window in the pediment of the roof. The fortified walls are battlemented and a door closely planked. A wooden framework seems prepared for a *cataracta.* On another part of the wall are frames of wood for some similar purpose.

LXXII.—*Fortification constructed by Decebalus.*

The Dacian king has provided a place of great strength from which to watch the Romans, and in which he can take refuge in necessity. It has triple lines of wall in the manner of Roman fortresses of the strongest kind. A man wearing the Dacian cap, probably Decebalus, points the way through one of the gateways, and several men are hurrying in, others are entering another gate, which appears to lead to a lofty acropolis, and a rock is seen in the foreground, on which two chiefs are standing, rallying the fugitives who are filling the courts and enclosures. They are retreating before the victorious legionaries after an action to be described in the next composition.

LXXIII.—*Attack of a Roman fortification.—Battle and defeat of the enemy.*

A strong place on high ground garrisoned by Roman soldiers. They have been attacked by a large body of Dacians, as is evident from the number of dead in this and of fugitives in the last composition. There are two gateways to the fort, and the Romans, not satisfied with repelling the attack on their walls, sally forth, sword in hand, and a desperate battle, partly from the walls, partly under them. The ground seems to be disputed valiantly by the Dacians, one of whom faces the rush of a host of Romans who fling themselves on the attacking force with immense energy. They are cutting, not stabbing, with their short swords, and some are using the *hasta*. All have oval shields. In some instances those of Romans and Dacians are ornamented alike. The field is covered with the enemy's dead and wounded, though he still makes head in portions of the field. From this disastrous encounter Decebalus leads the remnants of his army to the strong works seen in the last composition.

LXXIV.—*Another Roman fortress attacked by the enemy.*

Three walls are seen in this composition, and the determined assaults made on other strongholds seems to have necessitated the erection of walls of great strength by the emperor. These walls seem to be parts of a large circuit not yet completed, for we find in the furthest or left-hand part of the composition Roman soldiers fighting with their common *secures*, axes used for shaping timber. Trajan, too, is seen behind some rocky ground in the space between the second and third wall. The Dacians attack with the utmost determination. Some are seen beyond the first wall, and others have penetrated beyond the second. The Romans fight furiously in both these intramural spaces. Apparently the danger is so great that Trajan mounts his horse, and gallops off in person to bring up reinforcements. Numbers of Dacians are - dead and wounded in all parts of this broken ground. One is seen, a prisoner, thrust forward by the hair of his head in the direction of Trajan, who turns to question him, and whose communication probably leads to the action taken by the emperor.

LXXV.—*Trajan rescues his men with cavalry.*

By a valley among the rocks, on some of which his fortifications are in course of construction, the emperor comes to the rescue not a moment too soon. He is in armour, but is without a weapon. He rides at the head of his men, who come up at the gallop. Officers of heavy infantry can be distinguished by the plumes of their helmets behind the rocks in the background. How these troops, being cavalry, are to operate is not so clear, as the fighting is carried mainly under or between the various lines of circumvallation described in the last composition. Probably he makes the circuit of the unfinished walls, and falls on his enemy in the open.

Further are seen the tents and circumvallations of an entrenched camp. The general form is a semicircle. The right side of the enclosure is straight. It is semicircular on the other side.

LXXVI.—*The Bridge.*

In the foreground is a crowd of personages standing on the banks of the Danube which flows behind. The background of the whole composition being formed by the bridge, which I shall presently describe.

The Emperor Trajan appears more than once among the figures here represented, and they must therefore be taken to represent different actions, though they are so combined as to make the artist's intention in this arrangement a little obscure. First, Trajan marches at the head of his legionaries. He seems to have issued from the encampments behind. He is in full armour, and the *signiferi* and *imaginiferi*, with three standards, are behind him. These standards differ from any we have met with in earlier scenes, having *rostra* or ships' beaks represented on portions of their ornaments, decorated with ornaments showing the connexion of the legion with some naval exploit.

The emperor appears to be speaking, and points with the forefinger of his right hand in the direction of the bridge. He is probably explaining to them the necessity or advantage of this construction. His men are armed, and carry their shields and the helmets slung over the shoulder on the march.

Another action of this composition is represented. The emperor is offering sacrifice. He is dressed in a loose gown (*manicata*) with long loose sleeves which contract at the opening for the wrists. It is drawn up, and girt round the loins, the upper portion falling in ample folds below the cincture.

Behind these groups is seen one of the bridges built by Trajan over the Danube, which flows between it and the personages engaged on these various actions. About one fourth of the entire structure, as it is described by Dion Cassius, is here represented. On the right or south bank the approaches to the river bank are given. Two arches of masonry, the one nearest the bank lower and less in span than the further of the two. The masonry above the smaller is in mass sufficient to bring it up to the level of the road above. Water flows under the larger arch, and probably the river is supposed to rise

L 2

during the rains, and flow under the nearest as well. The larger arch abuts on the first large pier, built fairly in the bed of the river. The first pier rises to a considerable height out of the river. The height is described by the historian as 170 Roman feet. The top finishes with a projecting impost of stone, and there is a string course two courses of masonry lower. The other piers have the impost course only. All are represented as of hewn stone. The arches and the road above are of timber.

The thickness of the piers is represented by the historian as 60 Roman feet, and the distance from pier to pier as 170.

Over each pier are erected two pairs of strong shears of timber. The legs of each set are kept apart by rows of logs laid together the long way of the pier, and transverse timbers from leg to leg hold them all firmly together. Upon the legs of the shears abut arched girders composed of three concentric sets of beams tied to each other in three places by struts or ties, making altogether an arch, of which the curve is the fifth part of a circle. Horizontal beams rest on the points of junction of the shears from which they reach to the crowns of the timber arches.

Fig. 29.

On the horizontal girders which touch, and are supported by the crowns of the timber arches and the summits of the shears alternately, are laid cross beams or joists. Above these are a pair of latticed girders, one each side of the bridge. On the lower member of these and on the cross timbers or joists the road is laid. We are shown both girders in perspective.

It is stated by Dion Cassius that all the piers and arches were of hewn stone. If so, they are not shown in this view, nor on coins which bear this bridge on their reverse side.

The spot at which Trajan passed the Danube to penetrate into the heart of Dacia was at a short distance below the pass known as the iron gates, at which the river bends

at a right angle to the north and after a short distance
as suddenly to the south before resuming its western
course below the modern Gladova. The emperor must
have passed the river before the desperate engagements
described in previous compositions, and this representation
of the bridge is independent of the course of history.

LXXVII.—*Embassy of Dacians and others to the emperor.*

The scene is laid outside a Roman colonial station.
Several buildings are enclosed within a circular wall. An
amphitheatre made of timber is outside this enclosure,
arches are formed round the exterior, and a row of triangular window lights a corridor behind the upper seats.
From this a roofed passage communicates with a small
house placed at right angles to it. An open corridor
makes a communication with this and with another building, beyond which last is a triumphal arch with a flat
roof, and two military trophies above it. From this arch
issues soldiers in full marching order, and pass over a
wooden bridge, the first part of the parapet of which is
made of close palings.

The emperor, in civil costume, wearing the same sleeved
dress and boots and his *pallium*, stands in front of the buildings described. He is attended by several officers in the same
dress. The native ambassadors are of various tribes and in
various dresses. Some are such as we have already seen
on the Dacians. Two men in front of the emperor wear
light pantaloons gathered in puckers round the waist. The
upper part of the body is clothed only with a square
mantle clasped over the shoulder and half covering the
back and breast. The speaker wears a handkerchief
knotted round his head. One other man dressed in this
way wears a sheepskin cap. Another has some tight tunic
or jacket besides. Three men, of whom two are in the foreground, are dressed in long gowns gathered in the waists,
and with full skirts falling to the feet, altogether like a
modern woman's gown; but the breast and back are tightly
fitted with what appears to be plate armour; the plates
fastened together, and having the character of Asiatic plate
armour, such as is still used and continues to be made in
parts of India. Their dresses have tight sleeves to the
wrists, and their hands are in gloves. On the side furthest
from the emperor are two Dacians in pantaloons, gowns,
and cloaks; one wears a straight sword at his left side.
Both have high sheepskin caps, and hold their horses as

if about to mount after an unsuccessful interview with Trajan. Behind the emperor and his officers are armed Roman guard, and soldiers, and colonists in civil dress.

The ambassadors have no success with the emperor, who seems to reproach them with having violated the conditions imposed at the end of the war.

LXXVIII.—*March of the legionaries.*

From the archway described, the army of the emperor is again set in motion. It is not clear which of the two bodies in which the Roman army moved forward to attack the Dacian capital is here represented, that led by the emperor in person up the course of the Tjerna by the rocky pass abutting on the Danube at the iron gates, or the larger body sent by him down the Danube as far as the confluence of the river Aluta, with directions to march up the valley through which that river flows.

The legionaries cross a bridge over one of the rivers flowing along the respective valleys through which each army passed. At the head of the line of march marches the emperor himself in full armour, followed immediately by a figure dressed in civil costume, wearing a sleeved tunic, and over it the *paludamentum* or military cloak. This figure has been supposed to represent Hadrian, the successor of Trajan, who accompanied him in this second Dacian expedition, and who specially represented a policy of peace. The background consists of a lofty bank or cliff of rock, possibly representing the narrow defile leading northwards from the iron gates, or scenery meant by the sculptor to be suitable to such a route. Trajan is again represented on horseback. The emperor holds up his right hand with which he salutes the soldiers seen in the next composition, who are on the look out for his arrival.

LXXIX.—*Welcome of the emperor celebrated by a sacrifice.*

Trajan has hurried on at the head of his troops to reach a colony. Two groups of buildings are seen in the background. One is a square fortified camp. It has a tower of wood with a wooden railing or parapet on the top at one angle. A gate of which the side jambs or piers are finished with caps is covered by a pediment. The walls are battlemented, they have no buildings inside and defend a height. Adjoining this is a double colonnade covered with a roof.

The columns are of the Ionic order, and stand on a continuous base. Further on is a circular *prætorium,* within which a large tent is pitched. The *vallum* or wall is battlemented, and an arched gateway with a raised stone panel or square space above.

At the colony or station in which these buildings are represented Trajan meets the remainder of his army, perhaps that portion which is supposed to have marched up the valley of the Aluta, and with which he makes a junction at this point in order to make a combined attack on the capital and stronghold of Decebalus. The number of standards shows that this is an important section of his army. The prefect of the prætorians, with a crowd of officers and legionaries, are assembled to meet the Emperor.

LXXX.—*Another sacrifice.*

After the first lustral sacrifice a more solemn sacrifice is prepared within the circular prætorian quarters, shown in the background in the last composition. Tents are seen within the enclosure, and a bulging piece of wall or hollow tower on one side, perhaps represents the prætorian gate. Inside is seen the emperor dressed in the cinctus gabinus. He is pouring a libation from a patera in his hand.

LXXXI.—*Trajan addresses his troops.*

After the sacrifices are over the emperor, according to his custom, makes a speech to the legionaries, explaining the nature of the operations to be undertaken, and encouraging them against the difficulties in store in forcing their way through a warlike population. He is attended by two generals, one on each side, and by a lictor with the fasces. Two men, wearing the chain mail notched at the bottom and the military *pallium,* hold two horses, trapped and furnished with saddlecloths, and with oval shields hung on the left sides of the saddle coverings. These are the horses of the officers in attendance on the emperor.

LXXXII.—*Trajan sets his army in motion.*

The Emperor is seated on a stone *suggestum* or seat within the prætorium. This is represented as an enclosure of masonry, with a bead moulding on the top of the wall and hollow round towers formed at intervals along its course.

Two tribunes are beside him, each attended by an officer, of whom one is covered by his *pallium.* A *draconifer,* with his cohort standard, is also within the enclosure. Both the general officers hold their swords in their hands, one having his shouldered and holding it by the scabbard and hilt as prepared for an immediate advance. The men wear their helmets. In the background sumpter mules and a cart drawn by two horses are laden with armour, going forward for the use of reinforcements, sent on or expected to fall in on the line of march.

LXXXIII.— *The emperor provisions the stations on his route.*

Trajan is here seen at the head of the column of march. He is supposed to have brought the two divisions of his army into communication with each other.[35] They are represented in two lines, one behind a line of rocks or mountains. He appears in this composition at the head of one, perhaps Hadrian at the head of the other. Those behind the rocks are headed by *cornicines* blowing their instruments. Trajan and one officer are at the head of that column. He points to a circular wall or enclosure which is being provisioned. Most of the men heading the column wear crowns of olive or bay leaves round their helmets. They are headed by three ensigns. Nearest the column is an *aquilifer.* The emperor points to the entrance to the enclosure, before which stands a sentry. In the enclosure two carts, one drawn by one mule, a vicious animal with his ears back, and one by two horses, are loaded with sacks of grain and provisions, and these are in process of unloading by soldiers told off to that duty. One of the carts seems to hang below the axles. A soldier in the foreground kneels on a piece of rock, and dips with a long handled pot into the river. A small detached circular enclosure seems to be built on the level of the river. It has two tall wooden gates. The walls are battlemented.

LXXXIV.—*The advance continued.*

The army again advances. Nor does it, or portions of it, seem to have halted longer than was required for the purposes just explained.

---

[35] Following the routes named in the Introduction, pp. 81, 82.

Two lines or columns are again separated by rocky ground, and seem to be marching parallel to each other. In the background are seen the emperor leading, then a prætorian officer, an *aquilifer, draconifer* and an *imaginifer,* with their several standards representing the divisions of the legion. All the men of this, the reserved, force carry their helmets. The foremost column consists of auxiliary forces in the van, followed by light armed Romans. The line is led by archers in conical helmets, light cuirasses of linen, and long skirts reaching to the feet. They are armed with bows and arrows. After them come Germans followed by slingers, then come the Romans. It is probably for such native troops as have been enlisted on the line of march that helmets, shields, &c. have been seen sent forward as baggage.

LXXXV.—*Provisioning a station.*

A fortified camp or station of considerable extent is seen on the rocks in the foreground and running round the heights in irregular form. Tents are seen within. Inside the prætorian quarters, the nearest portion, a figure, Trajan or a prætorian officer, gives orders to two *cornicines* who sound accordingly. The men are ordered out to forage. They are seen outside cutting wheat in the fields with sickles, and carrying it in sheaves on their shoulders. One man within the prætorian quarters starts out armed with his dagger or sword for this purpose. Other men take out and pasture the mules. The mules are bridled and have a strap down the front of the nose joining the nose band with the forehead piece. A soldier is beating one of them. Another soldier is jamming back the bit in a mule's mouth, and the animal raises its head to the utmost reach of the neck to get out of reach of such punishment.

LXXXVI.—*A Dacian fortress.*

The Dacian fort is built on the summit of a rock, and follows the line of this elevated platform in a series of bold curves. A gate without defences is shown at a part of the wall. Dacians are watching outside. Two men, wearing the sheepskin cap and chiefs, are discussing the situation of matters. One, perhaps Decebalus himself, is apparently trying to give force to his orders. The other chief is remonstrating, and gives information as to the strength of the Romans. Common soldiers are with them, look-out men, and guards.

Inside the walls appear many Dacians in confusion having been driven in by or discouraged by the sight of the Roman army. The place is of importance, as we see in it several houses roofed and covered with skins, and having more than one story.

LXXXVII.—*Battle and defeat of the Dacians.*

A furious struggle is going on. The Romans engaged are the light troops only. The Dacians are fighting with great resolution. One in the centre of the battle is beaten down on one knee, but continues the struggle against a Roman. Another beaten to the ground seems to ask for quarter without effect. Another on one knee is seen stabbed down within the collar-bone. Others fight on more even terms, hand to hand. The ground is strewn with the dead of the enemy. In one part of the field they lie two deep, and the Romans stand on heaps of slain. A line of rocks protects a number of fugitives, who are seen hurrying in the direction of the fortress last seen. The Romans have suffered probably some losses in the action, and are seen occupying an entrenched camp from which they propose to issue in pursuit of the enemy, and from which the men and material for an assault on the capital are to be organised. This place is made as strong as possible. There appears to be two or more lines of enclosure. Within the second line are seen the tents of the prætorians.

LXXXVIII.—*Attack and assault of a Dacian fortress.*

The Dacians are collected in a large fortress constructed on the top of a rock. Part of it apparently excavated out of the rock itself at the angle nearest to the Roman post. A great length of wall is carried along the summit of the rock in irregular curves and lines suited to the shape of the ground. The wall is of cyclopian masonry, the stones large but not coursed. There are two courses of squared stones at intervals, and another on the crest of the wall, and these courses are ornamented with beads, or else these indicate parts tied in with timber, of which the ends are seen. The whole seems put together with great care. At two points, one a re-entering angle and the other the extreme outer angle in the face of the works, are two gates with towers built over them. The towers are roofed and a chamber, with a large square window, is over each gate. The gates are covered with plates of iron or skins nailed closely to the framework. A third gate where the wall falls back is similarly covered. A roofed gallery, the lower part between the posts that support the roof, protected by slabs of stone or plates of metal. The furthest, or left hand angle (spectators' right), is protected by a large round tower of squared masonry within which is a square watch tower with a door below and windows above.

The Romans make their first assault upon the right (spectators' left), where the fort abuts on the rock before mentioned. They try to carry this by escalade. Soldiers drag ladders up the rock to erect them against the walls, and from various levels make the same attempt. A number of slingers, both Romans and auxiliaries, are trying to beat ·off the defenders from their ramparts during these attempts. Others hurl the *pilum* or try to reach them with their spears. Several men have planted a ladder and hold it in place by main force. One brave man has mounted it, and from the upper round of the ladder cut off the head of one of the defenders. The defenders shoot arrows, strike down with spears and swords, and hurl large stones on the heads of the assailants. A young Dacian has fallen over from the walls and lies dead on a platform of rock close to a square well. Apparently, notwithstanding the determined nature of this assault, it is not successful.

LXXXIX.—*Siege and storm of the Dacian fort.*

The emperor and his immediate personal staff are standing on the low ground under the rock on which the fort is built. He has with him the main body of his army. He holds his sword sheathed in the hollow of his left arm, and receives from an officer an account of the failure of this first assault. He appears to be considering and discussing the best means for taking the place. On the height are a number of warlike engines that have been employed or are brought up in order to be employed in the capture of the fort. They are triangular frames consisting of three beams forming a triangle, the beams meet in a point and are fitted on the axle of a large wheel of solid timber. At the other end the three beams fit into the axle of a pair of wheels. A beam continued beyond the single wheel passes through a barrel or barrel-shaped mass and is prolonged beyond.

In the beam that forms the long axle are fitted handles for turning or straining ropes, and by the purchase obtained from this beam it seems the intention to raise the barrel, or cylinder in which sharpshooters can be raised above the breast of the wall, or combustibles can be thrown into the interior of the fort. The ends of the long axles that are nearest the wall are furnished with sickle-shaped iron tools, intended as boring implements to be worked by turning the axle by means of the handles described.

No covering of any kind is given to the machinery of these engines or to the workmen employed in them, as will be seen by the annexed woodcut. On the other hand it is more than probable that the sculptor shows us the skeletons and more solid parts only, the protecting work having been destroyed and the engines themselves, as indeed appears to be the case, abandoned. The height of the rock and careful construction of the works on this side make this a probable solution.

Fig. 45.

The first assault and such siege operations as have been conducted against these formidable works have failed or had only a partial success. Trajan seems to have determined on a fresh attack on the furthest and weakest angle of the fortress, which is protected by the tower of squared masonry already described. The gate of this work seems to have been forced. Judging from the care displayed in protecting other gates, this may be presumed to be a postern, or the position so difficult of access that less care has been taken in defending it. The whole angle at which this tower is built is invested on both sides by the forces of Trajan. The archers in mailed frocks and long skirts already described have climbed the rocks, and are pouring heavy discharges of arrows. The Roman soldiers advance covering their bodies carefully with their large shields, from behind which the deadly thrusts of their swords are aimed. They are supported by their comrades who strike over the heads of their friends with their long spears or hurl the *pilum* into the faces of the enemy. The Dacians fight from the walls. Some, bold from the previous failures of the Romans, rush from their stronghold in a vigorous sally, and with weapons and huge building stones try by main force to drive the Romans down the precipice. Meanwhile these latter have either found the postern in the round tower or followed the beaten party through it and are masters of this outwork. They send pioneers and others to the front. With *ligones*, axes, any weapon that comes to hand, they tear down the walls, and make breaches for their men, who protect them with shields and weapons during this work of destruction.

Within the place the enemy is utterly discouraged by this successful storm. The breaches in the tower make this angle and the entire place untenable. This, if not the capital of Decebalus, is his largest and strongest fort, and from this period of the war the resistance of the Dacians becomes hopeless. A number of Dacians look on apparently in despair.

XC.—*Trajan prepares stores of timber.*

The first care of the emperor after the capture of this important place is the preparation of stores of timber for building and for various constructions. The Romans are on the slopes of the Carpathians, and are near the retreat of the Dacian king. A number of men belonging to the heavy troops are cutting down large trees. The timber as it is cut is piled with perfect regularity in stacks. It is laid out at one place in the form of a circular bastion, behind which shelter can be found in case of any sudden attempts at interruption.

XCI.—*The emperor receives the submission of a native chief.*

The Emperor is attended by two general officers. In front of Trajan is a strong guard. They form two lines one standing on a ledge of rock above the other. They are prætorians, and are without their helmets.

A Dacian chief has been introduced into the presence of Trajan before whom he kneels on one knee. He is making signs of submission with his two hands, and looks up to implore mercy from the emperor. The emperor holds out his right hand, and appears to sign to him to rise.

XCII.—*Destruction of a large town by the defenders.*

A town of great size and strength. It is surrounded by walls, in some places double. Hollow semicircular towers are seen at intervals, and gates defended by towers and covered with skins or plated with iron. Roofed buildings of various sizes are seen inside the walls, some in two stories. Two round buildings can be distinguished, one in two stories. Both have conical roofs surmounted by a carved ball. All seem made of timber and covered with planks, nailed on. The inhabitants are setting fire to these buildings, apparently in despair of escaping capture and slavery. Next, the chiefs, to avoid the ignominy of captivity, take poison. One young man is received dead in the arms of his friends, and an old chief in a sheepskin cap stretches out his arms to take part in bearing so precious a burden. Others turn away and press their hands against their heads, sharing this despair. Another chief is dying, and a number more with and without caps stretch out their hands towards a chief, who has a cauldron before him, from which vials are being filled with the fatal draught. A man of similar rank beckons to or reproves a crowd of fugitives for not sharing in this act of self immolation. A father weeps over a dead son. Numbers lie dead already.

At the sight of this tragedy the crowd of fugitives, among whom are armed men and the bearer of one of the Dacian dragons, fly in horror, which is attested by their raised hands and gestures. They hurry out by a square gate in the furthest angle of the town. The angle of the opening in the inner wall by which one young man is flying is defended by one of the circular towers with conical roof, such as have already been described.

XCIII.—*Submission of a portion of the Dacian force.*

The emperor is surrounded by tribunes and prætorian officers. The Dacians kneel before him, and with eager gestures seem to excuse their conduct, offer submission, and implore his protection. He holds his sword by the hilt, the hilt being towards the suppliants, while his right hand takes hold of his *paludamentum*. This is interpreted by some critics to mean a refusal to hear them, and to signify the intention of advancing notwithstanding this submission. The sounding of the horn certainly favours this notion. On the other hand it is against all accounts of the humanity and political sagacity of Trajan to refuse a submission if made in good faith.

It is probable that, granting these persons their lives on certain conditions, he has announced his purpose to beat down all opposition to his authority, and that he refuses any general peace so long as a Dacian army of any kind keeps the field.

XCIV.—*Distribution of corn to the legionaries.*

The emperor distributes rewards to his soldiers in the shape of allowances, *annonæ*, of corn. The scene is a space outside the *prætorium* of a Roman encampment. The place is an old Dacian *oppidum*, the same that has already been represented as the capital, or one of the capital towns of Decebalus. In the right-hand angle, high on a point of rock, appears a fountain or natural well. It is arched over, a basin is formed in the recess by building up a wall to the spring of the arch, and a channel of stonework has been made to bring the water into the town.

A number of soldiers are carrying their allowances in large sacks, which are filled from a *modius*, a wooden vessel, hooped, containing something under two gallons (1·92) of our measure. The sacks are full and heavy, and are carried on the shoulder, the men grip the mouth of the sack with one hand, and the weight of the grain falls to the two ends; the opening in the middle requiring to be held carefully.

XCV.—*The emperor makes a speech to the troops.*

The imperial tent and two others are pitched in the prætorium quarters. They are carefully corded over, and ample curtains hung to the ends of these ropes or to poles of wood, which distend the tent cloths, conceal the entrances. Those of two tents are gracefully looped up, a valance cut into large round notches, with tassels between, hangs on the sides of these tents to protect the line of junction of the walls and roofs. Trajan is attended by a prætorian officer (perhaps by Hadrian). He holds his sheathed sword by the hilt, and his right hand is extended in the action of laying down decisions or rules of guidance. He is surrounded by tribunes and *signiferi*. The hearers of all ranks extend their right hands to signify their acceptance of these orders, and to pledge themselves to observe them. At the same time a number of light armed men are sent forward by the prætorian gate to protect the working parties.

XCVI.—*Additional fortifications.*

Great additions are made to this station by Trajan.
At a small distance another permanent fortification is
being built up. It is in several detached portions or divisions, each enclosed in a separate wall. Two on the right
hand appear to touch each other. One contains the prætorian quarters and tents. It is defended by battlemented
walls, and the entrances are placed in a semicircular recessed
wall.[36]

The gate being at one of the points of junction of the
semicircular wall with the line of fortifications, so that
it can be assaulted only by the number of men that the
space occupied by the recess can hold. Two *signa* are planted
in the prætorian enclosure.

In the second division of these fortifications are carts
laden with casks. The carts are on two wheels, the bodies
of the carts shallow and balanced above the axletrees. Men
are felling timber, and laying the masonry of this part of
the fort, and guards belonging to the same class of troops
told off for that duty are mounting guard over the armour
and arms, and protecting the working parties.

XCVII.—*Trajan rejects offers of submission.*

The emperor stands with his hands in the same action
as in No. XCIII. Two officers are beside him. One seems
to point to the suppliants, while pointing out their guilt.
Three Dacian chiefs are before him. One kneels, and the
three stretch their arms out to imply submission and ask
for mercy. The second prætorian officer, who is behind the
emperor, gives orders to the light troops. A third portion
of the new fortifications is seen in the background.

XCVIII.—*The light troops cross a temporary bridge.*

The orders of one of the prætorian officers has set in
motion a portion of the Roman troops. They cross a stream.
The bridge is formed by driving piles into the bed of the
river and laying timbers on them, with a road of planking
nailed thereon. The piles are three together in the deeper
and more rapid portions of the stream, and two together
as they near the opposite shore. The heads of the piles
meet in one large transverse timber laid in the direction
of the stream, and the planks are laid across from one of
these to the other. This bridge is identical in construction
with the bridge thrown by Julius Cæsar across the Rhine,

---

[36] See p. 56 of the Introduction.

and of which detailed drawings are given by A. Palladio.[37] This stream appears to be a tributary to a considerable river.

XCIX.—*Timber stores and fortifications abandoned by the Dacians.*

A wall, in two parts, perhaps signifying a double wall, defends a Dacian station, in which are piled great stores of timber. The logs are laid in rows longways and across, alternately, in the Roman fashion. The walls defending this space appear only on the side facing the spectator. The stream protects another side and a space of some distance on the only other side seen divides it from a Roman dock-yard established for the construction of boats. Water perhaps intervenes. These stations seem both to be at the foot of or near to spurs of the Carpathians, and close to a country well furnished with timber; the imperial forces as well as the enemy, having stores of this description at no great distance from one another.

From this fortified wall the Dacians are issuing giving and receiving orders, and encouraging each other to advance against the Roman station or one of their fortresses.

A Roman naval building yard is in the further background or left hand corner. Great stores of wood are piled round it, and soldiers, artificers, are seen with mallets and chisels at work on the construction of a boat. They wear their helmets during this operation, and the place is, perhaps, dangerously open to attack.

C.—*Attack on a Roman fortification.*

The Dacians attack a fort garrisoned by a detachment of imperial troops. They are in great numbers and swarm round the place on every side. They attack with arrows, lances, and weapons of all kinds. The place is on the top of a rock, and the enemy presses up the sides with great determination. The Dacians seem to attempt to form the combined movement of the Roman *testudo*, but their shields are oval and do not fit. They fall in great numbers, but press on without hesitation. Numbers of the dead of the enemy encumber the slopes of the rock below the scene of the chief fury of the assault.

The Romans defend themselves with desperate energy. Some thrust with spears, leaning over the walls to strike. Most of the defence is with large squared stones, by which we may conclude that the fortifications are still in progress.

Three gates can be made out. One of these constructions shows a long protruding beam pushed over the wall. From the end of it is hung by a chain the body of a Dacian chief killed on the crest of the wall. The great loss of life seems to have its effect on the Dacian army.

CI.—*The siege raised by the Dacians.*

The town is seen in the distance. It is walled and an opening in the walls signifies, though it does not represent, a gateway. There are buildings within the walls, one is a long narrow one storied house. The Dacians retreat amongst the hills. The greater number seem to be discouraging one another. Three chiefs in sheepskin caps remain to the last, looking back to the walls they have left, loth to go, but seeing that success is hopeless.

CII.—*Speech of Trajan and distribution of plunder.*

The emperor stands on a low *suggestum.* Two officers are behind him. In front of him are two standard bearers. Other officers and guards surround the emperor. Behind the guards come soldiers leading sumpter horses laden with paniers filled with cups, vases, and other precious objects. These, according to Dion Cassius, the historian, were found in a depository under the bed of a stream. This receptacle was prepared by the prisoners of Decebalus, who turned the course of the river Sargetia at a spot not far from his own stronghold. All the prisoners acquainted with this proceeding were put to death by Decebalus to prevent the possibility of this secret being divulged. Beculus, one of the number, alone survived and brought to Trajan such information as led to the recovery of the treasure. Part of this plunder is distributed by the emperor among the legionaries, and part secured for the use of the military chest. One soldier points to the emperor, apparently praising his generosity. Others turn back to look at the retreating forces of the enemy as he makes his way over the mountains.

CIII.—*Last address of Decebalus and his self-destruction.*

This and the following sculptures of the spiral give us the closing scenes of the war. Decebalus and his chiefs are in a wooded defile of the rocks. A figure on the right is probably Decebalus himself. He is haranguing his veterans.

The man next him wears a fringed *sagum*, and raises his
right hand with a gesture of high resolve. On a rock
above them other chiefs seem to hold a like debate. One
or two turn with apparent horror and amazement from the
only solution offered by Decebalus, to free themselves from
disgraceful bonds and captivity, that of self immolation.
To the left the king is seen again, he kneels on one knee
and with a dagger in his right hand raised above his head
is in the act of giving himself the fatal stroke. One chief
lies already dead. Another is sacrificing a friend who
kneels to receive his last blow. A few seem to escape
horrorstruck to tell the news to their friends, and to offer
the submission of hopeless men to the Romans.

CIV.—*The emperor receives news of the death of king Decebalus.*

Trajan in full armour is standing at the prætorian gate of
his quarters. A semicircular enclosure behind him contains
the imperial tent, with the entrance and curtains looped up.
The prætorian officers are behind him, and armed guards in
attendance.

One Dacian chief is introduced within the prætorian
enclosure, and kneels before the emperor protesting his submission with the action of his hands. Others are outside,
and with the right arm extended announce, no doubt, the
catastrophe just described. All wear the sheepskin cap,
and are chiefs. One bears in his left hand a dish containing
precious caskets and treasures.

The Roman cavalry are sent in pursuit of the relics of the
Dacian army. There are still bands of cavalry in the field,
and the emperor launches his own in pursuit. A strong
force of mounted knights are charging at the galop in
pursuit of the enemy. The action of the hands and arms
shows that some carry the lance across, some to the right
of their horses' necks ; some brandish it over head holding
by the middle in the fashion of modern Arabs. A fugitive
Dacian turns to watch the points of a weapon behind him.
Perhaps these are occasionally hurled forwards. But it is
more probable that a mounted warrior would not part with
so valuable a cavalry weapon. One man in the foreground has lanced the Dacian before him. This unfortunate
warrior is falling backwards from his horse, which is raised
back on its haunches by the movement. The scene is along
a mountain pass between rocks and among trees. The
pursuit progresses higher and higher amongst the hills.

As the pursuit advances the fugitives are overtaken by both cavalry and infantry, who fall in from passes in the hills. It is evident that the forces of Trajan have been sent in various directions so as to scour the ranges of hills, stop the passes, and completely hunt out the enemy wherever he continues to resist. Roman cavalry are here entering from a side opening in the hills, and infantry are further in advance having, as may be supposed, climbed places inaccessible to horsemen. The Dacians stretch their hands out, and seem to exhort each other to escape as they can. A Roman officer, with his hand pointing in advance, hurries up his men. Dacian dead are seen on the ground still with a grip of their shields, and a curved sword lies on the ground near one. The dead wear caps.

CV.—*Capture of a Prisoner of Rank.*

A Dacian of high rank is unhorsed, and lies on the ground beside a tree half supporting himself on his left arm. He has lost his shield, but grasps the scimetar in his right hand and glares fiercely on his pursuers. He is surrounded by Roman horsemen. One raises his lance to give him the finishing stroke. Another leans over his horse trying to secure him as a prisoner. A third has turned and leans with his body stretched over to his horses' head. He holds up the first and second fingers of the right hand offering quarter to the fallen man. Another infantry soldier has caught the horse by his bridle, and turns calling to the Dacian to surrender. The shield is richly ornamented. The man wears the sheep-skin cap and is a person of rank. Bellori's suggestion, that it is Decebalus, is inadmissible, as the news of the suicide of Decebalus has been already given to the emperor, and this fact is historical. No such catastrophe is commemorated regarding this warrior, whose rank is probably one great inducement to the offer of mercy at the moment, that he may grace the imperial triumph in Rome. The infantry are seen binding the arms of captives and thrusting others forward by the hair. Two soldiers, one a tall mounted horseman, secures a Dacian boy who seems to implore his liberty in vain.

CVI.—*The head of Decebalus brought to the Roman quarters.*

The scene is the prætorian quarter of a Roman camp It is built on a height and a double wall protects one pre-

cipitous side. Within is a crowd of Roman soldiers with
their helmets off. Two light armed soldiers have just
come into camp, and bear in their hands the head of
Decebalus on a board. All heads are turned on this
ghastly trophy. The eyes are closed and the sheepskin
cap still covers the hair. The tent of the emperor is
behind the crowd, and the emperor has probably been first
presented with this visible evidence of the conclusion of the
reign of his enemy.

CVII.—*Capture of fugitives of rank.*

A party of infantry soldiers have pursued and hunted
out a number of fugitives of rank. The unfortunate
Dacians are surrounded, bound hand and foot, and carried
away. They seem to have resisted, and to be men
of great personal strength, judging by the number of
Romans engaged in the capture and the confusion attend-
ing this violent proceeding, which is admirably rendered
by the sculptor. The scene is high in a mountain range,
and various wild beasts are introduced to signify the danger
and difficulty of the ground. One of the animals is considered to be the *urus*, a wild ox or auroch mentioned in
Cæsar's War in Gall. Another is a red stag, and another
a wild boar.

CVIII.—*Capture of the last mountain stronghold.*

High up among the hills explored by the Romans is
a small hill fort. It is built of timber and defended by
stockades. One building only seems to be of masonry.
A mountain stream or torrent defends it on one side The
Dacians are overpowered by the Romans, and some are
killed. The rest are taken captive and the wooden houses
and defences are fired.

Over a dip in the line of hills in the horizon is seen the
bust of a goddess with her *amictus* blown in a graceful
circle round her head. She represents, perhaps, Luna, and
this attack is made by help of moonlight.

CIX.—*Transplantation of the inhabitants with their property.*

The emperor, having completed the operations of the
campaign, sends the natives away from the various settlements formerly occupied and fortified by Decebalus, and

plants colonists in their room, or in the various fortified
camps and *oppida,* which we have seen in course of construction during the entire progress of both his wars. These
stations remained at various convenient distances along
the three Roman roads made by Trajan, and the names are
known.[38]   The Dacian natives were transplanted to places
where they could be no longer a source of difficulty or
danger to the Roman colonists or the imperial government
at home.

Families are moving off, one father carries a little boy
on his shoulders. A father, mother, and several children
form one sorrowful group, and seem to lament this enforced
exile.   One of the boys drives the cattle belonging to the
family.   Great herds of cows, asses, and flocks of goats and
sheep are represented by animals of each species.   They
browse on the herbs and bushes as they move.   Amongst
the crowd of men many carry sacks containing their moveable property on their shoulders.   A number of Roman
colonists in civil dress, wearing the *pallium* and the Roman
sandals, are marching after to take up the various quarters
assigned to them.

---

[38] See p. 85.

GENERAL INDEX.

LONDON:

Printed by GEORGE E. EYRE and WILLIAM SPOTTISWOODE,
Printers to the Queen's most Excellent Majesty.
For Her Majesty's Stationery Office.
[1275.—50.—5/74.]

2092128R00103

Printed in Great Britain
by Amazon.co.uk, Ltd.,
Marston Gate.